The Green Slow Cooker

The Green Slow Cooker

Vegetarian and vegan meals all year round

Heather Whinney

Contents

About the Book 6

Light & Bright 18

Fresh & Fragrant 56

Comforting & Earthy 98

Warming & Hearty 142

In the Oven & on the Hob 186

Thanks 215

Index 216

About the Book

The slow cooker is more than just a kitchen appliance, it is your culinary confidant, allowing you to produce creative meals throughout the year. Very few cooking skills are required, and nor does it need the constant watchful eye of the cook. It really is the ultimate in hands-off cooking.

The recipes in this book were an exciting challenge to write. They are vegetarian and I wanted each recipe to be a stand-alone bold flavour dish. I aimed to create main meals as much as possible, requiring very little in the way of grains or rice to complete them, mostly to eliminate any extra cooking. Secondly, I wanted to show how the slow cooker can be used all year round, from the colder months when slow cooking comes naturally into its own through to the longer, warmer days when vegetables become less robust to reflect the weather and by nature require less cooking.

Whatever time of year it is, there is nothing more satisfying than knowing that you've got lunch or dinner sorted, and the slow cooker delivers this on so many levels. From pot to table, it is minimum effort from the cook for maximum results! Some recipes require a little more attention at the beginning and others benefit from an added flourish at the end. All have been thoughtfully developed so they are really well-flavoured.

Light & bright, fresh & fragrant

You don't want to spend hours over a hob when the warmer days are here and it's too hot to cook. The slow cooker is incredibly liberating and is the perfect solution to produce delicious dishes without breaking a sweat. You can still enjoy the freshness and vibrancy of vegetables as they mingle in a sauce, stock or oil.

Lighter, delicate vegetables require less cooking time to avoid losing both taste and texture. Tender vegetables such as asparagus, courgettes, spinach, cauliflower, broccoli and peas are often added into the recipes for the last 30 minutes of cooking, or layered so they can gently stew. However, if it is more convenient to add the vegetables all together, that is fine. There are no rules – there will just be a change in texture.

Comforting & earthy, warming & hearty

Slow cooking is synonymous with the winter months, with one-pot dishes being the ultimate in comfort food when the weather is cold. Hardy vegetables such as root vegetables, kale, cabbages and leeks are ideal for the slow cooker, resulting in intensely flavoured stews and casseroles. Simmered low and slow, the taste of the vegetables is wonderfully concentrated and some retain their sturdy texture.

The seasoning
Cooking vegetarian dishes in a slow cooker requires a little more thought as you are not relying on meat for flavour. You need good seasoning and a clever combination of ingredients. To get the best fragrance from spices, they are often dry-fried during the prep stage before being added to the pot. Fresh herbs can simmer in the pot and, for an extra boost of flavour, stir more in at the end. Once you've mastered your slow cooker, don't be afraid to experiment with different flavour profiles to keep things interesting.

The stock
Too much liquid is the biggest and most frequent mistake made with slow-cooker dishes. This is because slow cookers trap the steam in, so the liquid doesn't reduce as it would in conventional cooking.

Don't be tempted to add more stock or liquid at the beginning as it will greatly reduce the flavour. If later on the dish is looking dry, a little hot water from the kettle can be poured in to loosen the dish, but always be wary when adding.

The prep
Using your slow cooker gives you the advantage of prepping ahead when you have the time, either first thing in the morning before the hectic schedule of the day begins, setting for an overnight cook, or prepping leisurely at the weekend for a family meal or an entertaining dish.

Chop your vegetables to roughly the same size so they cook evenly and use fresh vegetables unless otherwise suggested, such as frozen peas or broad beans.

Most of the recipes in the book benefit from sautéing the onions and garlic first, and occasionally some of the vegetables, before adding them to the pot. The recipes differ in the prep, each one developed to elevate the flavour to the ultimate in deliciousness.

Plant-based protein
Plant-based protein is added to many of the recipes, such as beans, lentils, legumes and tofu. They are added for extra protein and fibre but also for bulk and flavour. For a complete slow-cooker meal, grains, such as rice, bulgur wheat or barley, are often used or suggested as a side serving.

Beans and pulses
Cooking dried beans in the slow cooker is a great option, not only because they are economical but also because they are richly flavoured and hold their shape.

You do not have to soak your dried beans before adding them to the slow cooker, except for red kidney beans and cannellini beans as these both contain toxins that may not be destroyed in the heat of the slow cooker. To rid these beans of lectin (that can cause stomach upset), soak overnight, then give them a 10-minute high boil before adding to the slow cooker.

For the beans that don't require soaking, not soaking may mean that they need a slightly longer cooking time in the pot until they are tender.

Combine different types of beans for added texture and nutritional variety.

There is a growing dietary trend of vegetarianism but also people looking to just increase the amount of plants in their own diet, or as a family. Using the slow cooker to cook vegetarian dishes is such a good option because it's a really forgiving way of cooking, which makes it perfect for the accomplished or novice cook. There is less precision required with vegetable cooking than there is for cooking meat as specific times and temperatures aren't as crucial. This makes vegetarian slow cooking far more straightforward. And the principle remains the same whatever you are cooking and whatever time of year it is: your food is left in the capable hands of your slow-cooker appliance, giving you the time to do something else.

All the recipes in the book were tested in an oval 3.5 litre-capacity slow cooker with an easy dial: Low – High – Warm and a ceramic pot and glass lid. This style is a budget buy, easy to wash and great for serving straight from pot to table.

Notes on recipes
* **Eggs:** free-range medium
* **Butter:** salted
* **Pepper:** black
* **Salt:** sea salt
* **Stock:** choose one that is not too salty or use vegetarian bouillon powder

Store-cupboard essentials for vegetarian slow cooking

A good mix of dried herbs: don't overuse them as they can overpower in a slow cooker.

A mix of spices: such as turmeric, cumin, paprika, sumac and chilli flakes – best to fry before adding to the slow cooker.

Pastes and sauces: tomato purée, mustards, soy sauce and stock.

Tinned/cartons and jars: tomatoes, full-fat coconut milk, passata, sun-dried tomatoes, capers, olives, vinegars and a selection of beans.

Dried foods: rice, bulgur wheat, spelt, pasta, a selection of beans and pulses and lentils.

Food safety
A slow cooker is a safe way of cooking food as long as it is used correctly. Food cooked on the Low setting is generally at a temperature between 79–93°C and the High setting is approximately 149°C. Both Low and High settings cook at a temperature high enough to kill off bacteria. The same principles of food safety as for all cooking, such as hand-washing and cleaning boards, apply to slow cookers.

Kit
Other than your slow cooker, very little equipment is required:

- **A heavy-based frying pan** for sautéing if your slow cooker doesn't have this setting.

- **Pot holders or oven gloves**, as the pot will be hot when you remove it to serve.

- **Metal tongs** can be useful if you wish to move food around with minimum disturbance.

- **Wooden spoon** for sautéing and the occasional stir in the slow cooker if called for.

- **Timer** if you have a basic slow cooker it may not have a built-in timer.

- **Ladle** and **large spoon** for serving.

- **Stick blender** to blend soup in the pot or use a blender.

- **Meal prep containers** for the fridge or freezer.

Converting cook times from High to Low
Slow-cooker brands state that most recipes can be converted to cook on either setting to suit your lifestyle. All slow cookers differ slightly, but as a general rule of thumb, I use the following formula:

High to Low = + 4
Low to High = − 4

3 hours on High = 7 hours on Low
4 hours on High = 8 hours on Low
5 hours on High = 9 hours on Low
6 hours on High = 10 hours on Low
7 hours on High = 11 hours on Low
8 hours on High = 12 hours on Low

NOTE: *The recipes in the book were only tested on the settings given for each recipe.*

Economical
Slow cookers are designed to cook food low and slow at a consistent temperature. They are very economical as they use minimal power due to the sealed pot with low-wattage coils, which consume low levels of electricity. On average, they use 200 watts (depending on the size of the pot), which draws about the same electricity as a standard light bulb. Running your slow cooker on Low for 8 hours is the equivalent of having the oven on for about 35 minutes. This makes the slow cooker a really energy-efficient choice and budget-friendly cooking method.

Cooking vegetarian food in the slow cooker allows you to easily put more good-value plants on your plate. Using affordable and accessible ingredients, vegetables that are in season and beans and pulses are all wise economical choices. Good for your wallet and your health!

Freezing
Cooking in the slow cooker is a super convenient way to get family meals on the table, but it's also a great way to batch cook for the freezer, so you can enjoy homemade food when time is short. This will save money and reduce kitchen waste.

Once food is cooked, remove the pot from the outer casing and allow it to cool slightly, then divide the food into suitable freezer-proof containers – it will cool quicker this way. When completely cold, seal, label and put in the freezer.

Not all the recipes will freeze well. It's best to choose casseroles, stews, soups and curries. Make sure all the vegetables are immersed under stock or sauce before sealing and freezing. These recipes will freeze for 3–12 months without a loss of quality.

Reheat and eat

Remove the meals from the freezer and allow them to defrost in the fridge overnight before reheating. To reheat in the microwave, heat for about 3 minutes until piping hot, then remove, stir and heat for a further 2–3 minutes, depending on the size of the containers. Do not reheat food more than once. Alternatively, reheat the dish in a pan on the hob until piping hot.

Cook once and eat twice: refrigerate and cover any leftover slow-cooker meals, put in the fridge within 2 hours and eat within 3–4 days. Reheat as above.

The slow cooker

All slow cookers work in essentially the same way, regardless of the size, style or design. There is an outer casing of usually stainless steel or enamel, which contains low-wattage heating coils (this is what allows the food to cook). This heats up slowly and gently and holds the heat at a constant level. There is then an inner container that fits snugly inside the outer casing, plus a lid, often glass, which traps the steam.

Choosing your slow cooker

There are a few things to consider before buying a slow cooker that will determine your choice, such as the shape, the amount of space you have on your countertop or in your cupboards, how much food you want to cook at one time and how high tech you wish to go. There is a slow cooker to suit every lifestyle and budget.

Size/Capacity

The main consideration when buying a slow cooker is how many people you need it to feed. Obviously, there are slight variations depending on the types of dishes you want to cook and appetites, i.e. a soup cooked in a 3.5 litre pot will easily feed 6, as would a curry, but certain vegetable dishes may only serve 4. As a guide:

- **Cooking for 1–3:** choose between a 1.5–3 litre pot

- **Cooking for 4–6:** choose a 3.5 litre pot

- **Cooking for 6 or more:** choose between a 4.5–7 litre pot

A large-capacity pot is also good if you want to use it for batch cooking and freezing.

A slow cooker uses between 50–300 watts depending on the model and size. So, the larger the pot, the higher the wattage and running costs.

Tech

Most slow cookers have three heat settings: Low, Warm and High. A keep-warm setting is a really useful function as it will

stop your food from going cold, but not overcook it if you are not ready to serve immediately. Choose from a simple dial to a higher-tech digital dial.

A timer option is a good feature if you are not going to be home when the food is ready as it will automatically switch to the Warm setting when the selected time has been reached.

Lots of slow cookers now have a sauté function within the inner pot, ideal for recipes that require this step so you don't have to use a separate frying pan. Sautéing before slow cooking is not essential but it certainly boosts flavour!

Price

The variety of design and technology is reflected in the price. Slow cookers can vary from simple budget-friendly options to high-tech versions that offer more than just slow cooking, and these appliances can cost into the hundreds. It's a personal choice, but things to consider are how often is it going to be used and how energy-efficient the model is.

Storage

The space you have in your kitchen may also be a determining factor in the choice of your slow cooker. Storing it in a low-level cupboard is preferable as the larger ones can be really heavy to handle if stored too high. The countertop is perfect if there is room and it is used regularly.

If you want to prep the raw vegetable ingredients and leave the pot overnight in the fridge before cooking, be careful to bring it up to room temperature before plugging the pot in to start cooking. The pot may crack if subjected to intense temperature changes.

Easy clean

A huge bonus of slow cookers is that they are easy to clean. Most pot inserts are glazed ceramic, making them the perfect take-to-the-table pot! The inner pots can be washed with warm soapy water using non-abrasive cleaners and most can be placed in the dishwasher. Never immerse the outer heating unit in water. Unplug, allow it to cool and wipe the exterior with a damp cloth.

One thing your slow cooker does really well is cook fluffy, delicious rice just like a rice cooker. Before we get into the main-event recipes, have a look at how to cook rice for simple, easy day-to-day accompaniments.

Perfect Rice in the Slow Cooker

White basmati rice

SERVES 4–6
PREP 5 MINS
COOK 2 HOURS ON HIGH

Knob of butter or a drizzle of olive oil (to stop the rice from sticking and add flavour)

500g basmati rice, rinsed
900ml water
Pinch of salt

Perfect fluffy rice every time!

1. Put the butter or oil in the slow cooker, then add the rice, pour in the water and add the salt.
2. Stir, put the lid on and cook for 2 hours on High. Check the rice is cooked and if it isn't quite tender, give it another 15–30 minutes.
3. Fluff up with a fork and serve as in the slow-cooker recipe.

Brown rice

SERVES 4–6
PREP 5 MINS
COOK 2½ HOURS ON HIGH

Knob of butter or a drizzle of olive oil
400g brown rice, rinsed
900ml water or vegetable stock (for more flavour)
Pinch of salt

Wonderfully tender and nutty!

1. Prepare and cook as for the white rice but for 2½ hours on High.

Wild rice

SERVES 4–6
PREP 5 MINS
COOK 2½ HOURS ON HIGH

Knob of butter or a drizzle of olive oil
250g wild rice
700ml water or vegetable stock (for more flavour)

Wild rice is actually a grass and has a slightly chewy texture. Serve on its own or cook and serve mixed with other rice or grains.

1. Prepare and cook as for the white rice but for 2½ hours on High.

Dos and Don'ts of Slow Cooking

 ## Do . . .

- ✔ Preheat the slow cooker before using. Do this on High while you do your prep.

- ✔ If you are out all day, choose recipes that don't need ingredients adding at a later stage.

- ✔ Choose a prep and set dish.

- ✔ For ultimate ease, prep everything you need the night before, leave overnight in the fridge, then throw it into the slow cooker in the morning ready to go.

- ✔ Get to know your slow cooker and be aware that slow-cooker brands differ in the temperature that they reach. The difference between the High and Low setting is not so much the temperature as the time it takes for the cooker to come up to a simmer point (the slow cooker cooks food at a low temperature – on average between 79°C and 140°C). Food takes about 7–8 hours to reach a simmer point on Low and about 3–4 hours on High.

- ✔ Always remember to switch the plug off at the mains once your slow-cooker meal is ready. It's easy to forget once you have removed your ceramic pot from its casing. And remember it remains hot to the touch for a while.

 # Don't . . .

- ✘ Don't remove the lid for at least the first 2 hours of cooking unless the recipe states to do so.

- ✘ If you lift the lid, you will need to add 20 minutes to the cooking time.

- ✘ Don't under-fill the slow cooker as the food could burn. And don't over-fill it or the food may overflow and it will take a lot longer to cook. Aim to fill the slow cooker about three-quarters full.

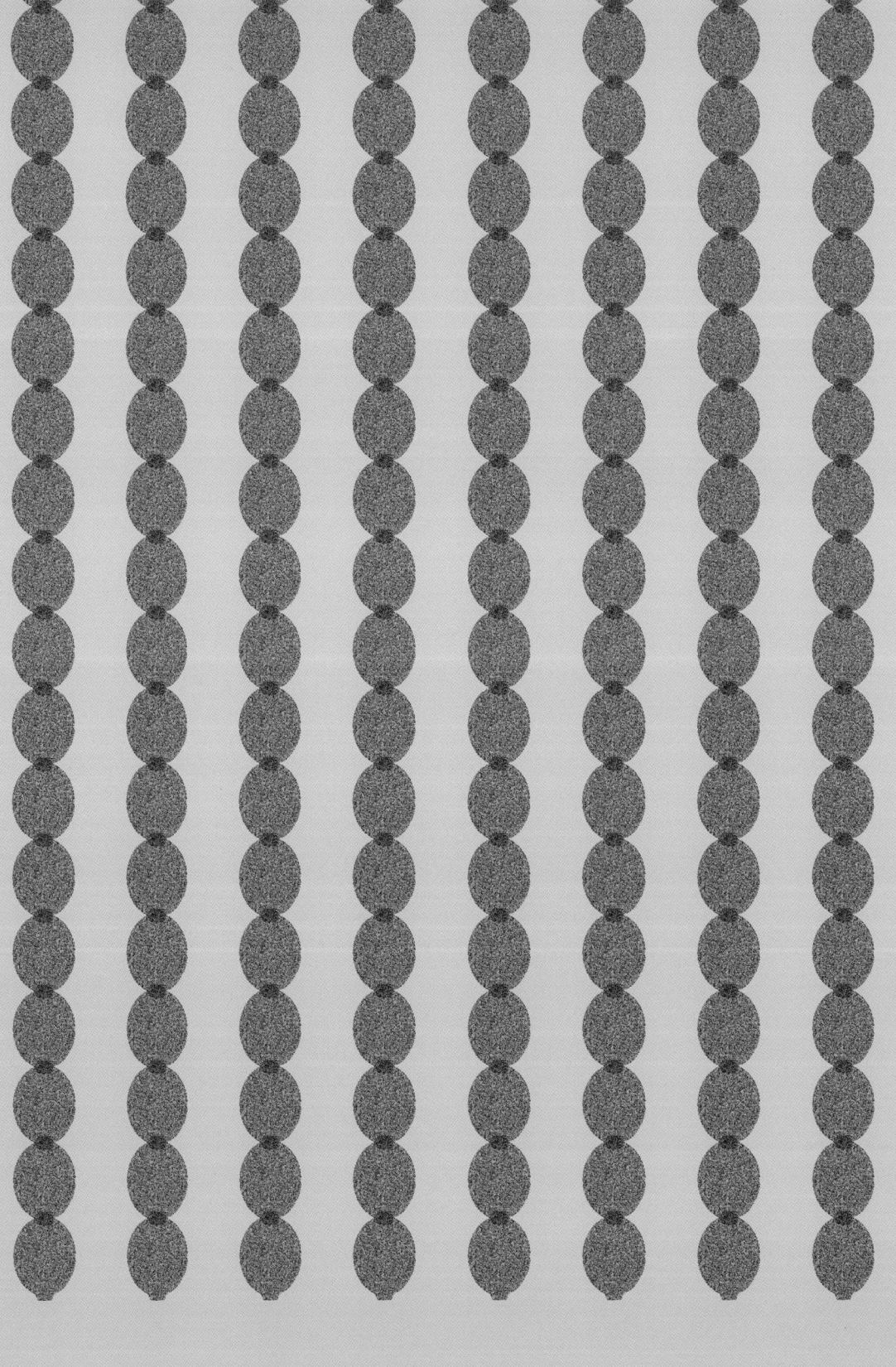

1.
Light & Bright

New potato and asparagus pot with goat's cheese

SERVES 4
PREP 15 MINS, PLUS 2 HOURS PICKLING
COOK 3¼ HOURS ON HIGH

1 tbsp olive oil
1 red onion, finely chopped
3 cloves garlic, finely chopped
Zest and juice of 1 lemon
1 green chilli, deseeded and finely sliced
2 tbsp capers
200g green beans, trimmed
Bunch of fresh dill, chopped
400g tin of cannellini beans, drained and rinsed
500g new potatoes, halved if large
500ml vegetable stock

Bunch of asparagus, woody stems trimmed (save the ends for soup)
200g peas, frozen or fresh from pods
285g jar artichokes, drained
Small bunch of mint, leaves picked and chopped
200g goat's cheese, crumbled or sliced
Sea salt and freshly ground black pepper

For the sweet onions
2 red onions, finely sliced
5 tbsp red wine vinegar
3 tbsp sugar

This is spring in a pot – a mix of tender, green vegetables and beans in a fragrant herby and lemony broth. Enjoy it on its own with some good crusty bread or spoon it over cooked bulgur wheat or rice.

1. Heat the oil in a large frying pan, add the onion and season well, then cook for 2 minutes. Stir in the garlic and lemon zest, cook for a few seconds, then add it all to the slow cooker.

2. Add the green chilli, capers, green beans, dill, cannellini beans, potatoes and stock to the slow cooker, then cover with the lid. Cook on High for 3 hours.

3. Meanwhile, make the sweet onions by adding the onions to a bowl with the vinegar and sugar. Stir until everything is well combined, then set aside for 2 hours to pickle.

4. After the slow cooker has been cooking for 3 hours, add the asparagus and cook for 15 minutes more until the asparagus is tender, then stir in the peas, artichokes and most of the fresh mint. Add a squeeze of lemon juice.

5. Remove from the heat, then top with goat's cheese and scatter with the remaining mint leaves. To serve, spoon over the sweet red onions.

Saffron rice with asparagus and dill raita

SERVES 4–6
PREP 5 MINS
COOK 2¼–2½ HOURS ON HIGH

500g basmati rice, rinsed well with cold water
100g butter, cubed
Generous pinch of saffron mixed with a little hot water
900ml water
Bunch of asparagus, woody stems trimmed (save the ends for soup)
Sea salt

For the raita
200g Greek yoghurt
Handful of dill, finely chopped, plus a few extra for garnish
½ cucumber, finely diced
Juice of 1 lemon

For the topping
200g pomegranate seeds
Handful of pistachio nuts, chopped (optional)

Rice cooks wonderfully in the slow cooker – really fluffy. Give it a good rinse first to remove the starch, then the grains will remain separate when cooked this way. This can be eaten on its own as a dish or served as a side dish.

1. Add the rice and butter to the slow cooker and season well. Mix in the saffron water and the 900ml of water and stir. Put the lid on, set the slow cooker to High and cook for 2 hours.

2. After the 2 hours, use a fork to fluff up the rice, then lay the asparagus on top and cook for a further 15–30 minutes until asparagus is cooked.

3. While it is cooking, prepare the raita. Mix all the ingredients together and season it well.

4. To serve, scatter the rice with the dill, pomegranate seeds and pistachios, if using, and serve with the raita.

Thai green curry

SERVES 4–6
PREP 15 MINS
COOK 5 HOURS ON HIGH

500ml vegetable stock
2 x 400ml tins of full-fat coconut milk
300g button mushrooms, halved
200g sugar snap peas or mangetout, finely sliced

For the green curry paste
1 tbsp olive oil
4 shallots, peeled, or use 1 small red onion, finely chopped
3 cloves garlic, roughly chopped
2 green chillies, halved and deseeded (leave the seeds in if you like the heat), finely chopped
5cm piece of fresh ginger, peeled and roughly chopped
1 lemongrass, trimmed and grated (a microplane works best)
1 tsp ground coriander
1 tsp ground cumin
2 tbsp dark soy sauce
Splash of mirin or Chinese rice vinegar (optional)
1 tbsp white miso (sweet)
Juice of 1 lime
1 tbsp demerara or soft brown sugar
Bunch of coriander, stems included, reserve a few leaves for garnish
Handful of Thai basil leaves (or use regular basil), reserve a few leaves for garnish
Sea salt and freshly ground black pepper

To serve
80g bunch of watercress, leaves only, washed
Chilli flakes (optional)
Few slices of lime

This recipe uses a home-made green curry paste. You can substitute it with a ready-bought one if you prefer, but check the label as most versions contain shrimp paste and fish sauce. The coconut milk is added for the last hour of cooking as it can easily split and spoil if it is cooked too long and slow. Do also use a full-fat one. Enjoy ladled over rice.

1. First, make the green curry paste. Heat the oil in a frying pan, add the shallots, season and cook for a minute, then stir in the garlic, chilli, ginger and lemongrass and cook for a further minute. Transfer the mixture to the slow cooker along with the rest of the paste ingredients.

2. Now add the hot vegetable stock, stir, put the lid on and cook on High for 4 hours.

3. After the 4 hours, add the coconut milk, button mushrooms and sugar snap peas or mangetout and cook for a further 1 hour.

4. To serve, stir through the watercress and top with the chilli flakes, if using, then garnish with the reserved coriander and basil leaves and the lime slices.

Singapore noodles with egg scramble

SERVES 4
PREP 15 MINS
COOK 2 HOURS ON HIGH

1 tbsp sesame oil
1 onion, roughly chopped
3 cloves garlic, sliced
2 sticks celery, finely chopped
5cm piece of fresh ginger, peeled and finely sliced
1 red chilli, deseeded and finely sliced
3 spring carrots, peeled and sliced into strips
2 red peppers, deseeded and sliced into strips
½ spring cabbage, shredded

3 tsp mild curry powder
300ml vegetable stock
1 tbsp Shaoxing rice wine or dry sherry
1 tsp demerara sugar
2 tbsp dark soy sauce
250g vermicelli noodles (4 blocks)
Sea salt and freshly ground black pepper
Chopped chives, to garnish (optional)

For the egg topping
25g butter
2 eggs, lightly beaten

This is a mix of spring veg and noodles in a light curry sauce, topped with scrambled egg, which is made quickly in a pan and added at the end. You can actually make scrambled egg in the slow cooker, but unless you need a huge amount, there isn't really the need.

1. Heat the sesame oil in a frying pan, add the onion, season well and cook, stirring, for a couple of minutes, then add the garlic and celery and continue cooking until just softened. Transfer the onion and celery mix to the slow cooker, then add the ginger, chilli, carrot, peppers and cabbage to the slow cooker.

2. Mix the curry powder with the stock and add, then stir in the Shaoxing rice wine or dry sherry, sugar and soy sauce. Put the lid on, set to High and cook for 2 hours.

3. Soak the noodles in boiling water for 2 minutes or as per the pack instructions, drain well, then stir into the vegetable mix.

4. To serve, heat the butter in a frying pan, add the egg and let it spread and cook for a few seconds. Push it around the edges with a fork, being careful to not over scramble it. When ready, lift it out, roughly chop and add to the top of the noodles dish. Garnish with chives, if using.

Sweet potato, spring cabbage and fennel pot with harissa and lemon

SERVES 4
PREP 20 MINS
COOK 6 HOURS ON LOW

1 tbsp olive oil
1 onion, finely chopped
3 cloves garlic, finely chopped
1 bay leaf
2 tsp za'atar
1 fennel bulb, trimmed and finely sliced, fronds reserved for garnish
1 pointed spring cabbage, trimmed and finely shredded
Zest of 1 lemon
1 tbsp tomato purée
1–2 tsp harissa paste (depending on how hot you like it and the brand you are using)
3 sweet potatoes, peeled and cubed
6 tomatoes, roughly chopped
500ml hot vegetable stock
Sea salt and freshly ground black pepper

To serve
2 tbsp tahini mixed with juice of 1 lemon and a pinch of salt (if it's too thick, let it down with a little warm water from the kettle and whisk)
2–3 tbsp Greek yoghurt
½ tsp harissa mixed with a little olive oil
Mint leaves
Lemon wedges

Spring and winter cabbage work so well in the slow cooker as they are hardy vegetables. Here spring cabbage is teamed with fennel to add a delicate aniseed flavour, harissa to fire it up a little and sweet potatoes to fill you up and add sweetness. This would be delicious served with warm pittas along with the tahini drizzle and yoghurt.

1. Heat the olive oil in a frying pan, add the onion, season well and cook for a couple of minutes. Stir through the garlic, bay leaf and za'atar and cook for a further minute, then add the mixture to the slow cooker.

2. Add the fennel, cabbage, lemon zest, tomato purée, harissa paste, sweet potato, tomatoes and stock to the slow cooker and give it all a stir. Put the lid on and set on Low for 6 hours.

3. To serve, drizzle over the tahini, yoghurt and harissa and garnish with mint leaves and lemon wedges. Serve with warm pittas or flatbreads.

Spring green minestrone with orzo pasta

SERVES 4–6
PREP 15 MINS
COOK 4 HOURS ON HIGH

1 tbsp olive oil
Bunch of spring onions, trimmed and finely chopped
3 cloves garlic, finely chopped
400g tin of cannellini beans, drained and rinsed
1 small spring cabbage/greens, trimmed and finely shredded
300g broad beans, frozen or fresh from pods
300g peas, frozen or fresh from pods
Piece of vegetarian Parmesan rind or use 2 tsp yeast flakes
Pinch of chilli flakes
800ml hot vegetable stock
Bunch of asparagus, woody stems trimmed (save the ends for soup), chopped into bite-sized pieces
200g orzo pasta (or snip spaghetti into small pieces)
2–3 tsp vegetarian basil pesto sauce from a jar
Sea salt and freshly ground black pepper
Grated vegetarian Parmesan, to serve (optional)

A super-simple green soup, full of vegetable yumminess and goodness. This is similar to the thick tomato version, just made without the tomato base and using green vegetables and broth. It's just as tasty with added tiny pasta and you can match your veg to whatever is available.

1. Heat the olive oil in a frying pan, add the spring onion, season well and cook for a few minutes to soften. Add the garlic and cook for a minute more. Transfer to the slow cooker.

2. Add the cannellini beans, cabbage/greens, broad beans, peas, Parmesan rind or yeast flakes and chilli flakes, then pour over the stock, stir and put the lid on. Set the timer for 4 hours on High.

3. For the last 30 minutes, add the asparagus and pasta, then stir through the pesto to serve. If you wish the soup to be slightly more liquid, top it up with a little hot water from the kettle and stir. Don't over-dilute the flavours though. Serve with grated Parmesan, if using, with crusty bread on the side.

Pearl barley risotto with courgette and tomato

SERVES 4
PREP 10 MINS
COOK 2½–3 HOURS ON HIGH

1 tbsp olive oil
1 red onion, finely chopped
3 cloves garlic, finely chopped
3 courgettes, trimmed and cut into chunky batons
1 green chilli, deseeded and finely chopped
1 tsp ground cumin
1 tsp sumac
2 tsp capers
2 tbsp sun-dried tomatoes, chopped
300g pearl barley
500ml passata
600ml hot vegetable stock
Sea salt and freshly ground black pepper
Flat-leaf parsley leaves, for garnish

Pearl barley makes a fabulous grain-based risotto, for flavour and texture. Here it is cooked with a heady mix of punchy flavours and is super versatile – eat hot as a supper dish, serve cold as part of a mezze-style lunch or with a salad, or it's delicious topped with a tangy cheese.

1. Heat the oil in a frying pan, add the onion, season well and cook for a couple of minutes, then stir in the garlic, courgette, chilli, cumin and sumac and cook for a couple more.

2. Transfer the mixture to the slow cooker and stir in the capers, sun-dried tomatoes, pearl barley, passata and stock. Put the lid on and set on High for 2½–3 hours until the pearl barley is tender and cooked.

3. Take a look in the last ½ hour to check if it needs topping up with a tiny bit more hot water from the kettle. Taste and season some more if needed. Garnish with parsley leaves and serve with a rocket and tomato salad.

Malaysian-style curry with sambal, aubergine and okra

SERVES 4
PREP 20 MINS
COOK 4 HOURS ON HIGH

2 tbsp olive oil
4 shallots, finely chopped
3 cloves garlic, finely chopped
1 red chilli, deseeded and finely chopped
1 lemongrass, trimmed and grated
5cm piece of fresh ginger, peeled and finely chopped
1 tsp cumin seeds and 1 tsp coriander seeds (crushed in a pestle and mortar)
2 tsp ground turmeric
2 tsp curry leaves, crushed between fingers
Zest of 1 lime (reserve lime for serving)
1–2 tsp sambal oelek (optional, add it for your heat preference)
300g mango pulp
400g tin of chopped tomatoes
300ml hot vegetable stock
Bunch of coriander, stalks finely chopped, leaves chopped (reserve a few whole coriander leaves for garnish)
2 aubergines, trimmed, quartered lengthways and halved (or use 6–8 small aubergines if you can get them)
175g okra, trimmed and sliced
Handful of cashew nuts, lightly toasted (optional)
Sea salt and freshly ground black pepper

For the cucumber pickle (optional)
1 cucumber, halved lengthways, deseeded and chopped
1 red chilli, deseeded and finely chopped
2 tbsp rice wine vinegar
Pinch of sugar

A sweet curry with hot notes, this is a rainbow of colour – great to serve at the weekend with rice and the cucumber pickle on the side. Not everyone loves okra. If you're not a fan, simply omit it from the shopping list and use green beans instead. This is great topped with sweet cashew nuts to serve but switch to your favourite – almonds would also be perfect.

1. Heat half the oil in a frying pan, add the shallots, season well and cook for a couple of minutes. Add the garlic, chilli, lemongrass and ginger and cook for a further couple of minutes. Stir in the cumin seeds, coriander seeds, turmeric and curry leaves and cook for a minute, then transfer it all to the slow cooker.

2. Add the lime zest, sambal paste, if using, mango pulp, chopped tomatoes, stock and coriander stalks, then stir in the aubergine. Put the lid on and set on High for 4 hours. When ready, stir through the chopped coriander leaves.

3. To make the cucumber pickle, toss the cucumber with the chilli, rice wine vinegar and sugar and stir until the sugar dissolves, then put to one side.

4. When ready to serve, heat the remaining oil in a frying pan and add the okra (frying them will prevent them from going slimy). Cook for 5–6 minutes until pale golden, then tip them into the slow cooker. Scatter over the cashew nuts, if using, and serve with rice and the cucumber pickle on the side.

Asparagus ends soup with soft-boiled egg and cress topping

SERVES 4
PREP 5 MINS
COOK 3 HOURS ON HIGH

Splash of olive oil
1 onion, chopped
3 cloves garlic, chopped
Bunch of asparagus ends (the woody ends that usually get discarded)
2 medium potatoes, peeled and chopped
2 spring onions, trimmed and chopped
1 leek, trimmed, washed and chopped
500ml vegetable stock
Drizzle of double cream, plus a little for garnish (both optional)
2–4 eggs (depending on appetite), soft-boiled, halved
Mustard cress, for garnish
Sea salt and freshly ground black pepper

This uses the woody ends from asparagus to make use of these leftovers, as they are so often just thrown away. You will need to pass the soup through a sieve after blending to get rid of any fibrous bits, but it still delivers on flavour!

1. Heat the olive oil in a frying pan, add the onion, season and cook for a couple of minutes. Stir through the garlic and cook for a minute more, then tip the mixture into the slow cooker along with the asparagus ends, potato, spring onions, leek and stock.

2. Put the lid on and cook on High for 3 hours. Stir through the cream, if using.

3. Stand the stick blender into the soup and blitz until smooth, then pour the soup through a sieve. Taste and season some more if needed.

4. Serve topped with soft-boiled egg and cress and a swirl of cream, if using. Enjoy with some sourdough bread on the side.

Brown rice and soya bean pilaf in a sweet Asian sauce

SERVES 6
PREP 15 MINS
COOK 2½ HOURS
 ON HIGH

1 tbsp olive oil
1 onion, finely chopped
3 cloves garlic, finely chopped
1 lemongrass, trimmed and grated
5cm piece of fresh ginger, peeled and grated
400g brown rice, rinsed
2 tbsp dark soy sauce
1 tbsp maple syrup
1 tbsp sweet chilli sauce, plus extra for drizzling
Juice of 1 lime
700ml hot mushroom or vegetable stock
300g frozen soya beans (or use broad beans or peas)
Sea salt and freshly ground black pepper
Large handful of pomegranate seeds, for garnish
Handful of mint leaves, for garnish

This isn't so much a sauce as a sweet and fragrant stock that the brown rice cooks in, and it marries so well. This can be served as a dish on its own or as an accompaniment to another dish. Pomegranates are added for a pop of sweet-and-sour flavour and colour.

1. Heat the oil in a frying pan, add the onion, season well and cook for a couple of minutes, then stir in the garlic, lemongrass and ginger and cook for a couple more minutes. Transfer the mixture to the slow cooker and stir in the rice.

2. Mix together the soy sauce, maple syrup, sweet chilli sauce, lime and hot stock, stir and pour it over the rice. Stir in the soya beans.

3. Put the lid on and cook on High for 2½ hours. Taste and season some more, if needed.

4. To serve, throw over the pomegranate seeds, drizzle over sweet chilli sauce and garnish with mint leaves.

Mediterranean layered savoury bread-and-butter bake with feta

SERVES 4
PREP 20 MINS
COOK 2 HOURS ON LOW

1 tbsp olive oil, plus extra for drizzling
1 red onion, finely chopped
3 cloves garlic, finely chopped
Large handful of basil leaves, torn, plus a few for garnish
6 chunky bread slices, lightly buttered
200g feta, cut into slices
250g cherry tomatoes, halved
400ml semi-skimmed milk
3 eggs
2 tsp dried oregano
Sea salt and freshly ground black pepper

This makes great use of leftover bread, and the other ingredients may be lurking around the fridge. It's like a baked version of a panzanella, the bread and tomato salad! You can vary your vegetables and cheese to suit, but make sure they are bold and gutsy as they need to cut through the egg custard mix. Really good served with a rocket salad.

1. Heat ½ tablespoon olive oil in a frying pan, add the onion, season well and cook for a couple of minutes, then stir in the garlic and cook for a minute more. Stir in the torn basil.

2. Drizzle the remaining olive oil in the slow cooker, then layer the bread with the onion mixture, feta and cherry tomatoes.

3. In a jug, mix the milk, eggs and oregano together and pour it over the bread layers. Push the bread down so it's all immersed under the egg mixture. Put the lid on and cook on Low for 2 hours.

4. Drizzle with olive oil to serve and garnish with basil leaves. Serve with rocket or a green leafy salad.

Hunter's rice with wild garlic

SERVES 4
PREP 5 MINS
COOK RICE 2½ HOURS ON HIGH/GARLIC 4 HOURS ON LOW

For the garlic
4 whole garlic bulbs, tops sliced off
Olive oil

For the rice
1 tbsp olive oil
1 red onion, finely chopped
2 sticks celery, finely chopped
400g brown rice, rinsed
50g butter
700ml hot vegetable stock
Large handful of wild garlic, leaves and flowers, rinsed, or use 220g baby spinach (wilted in the microwave)
200g frozen peas (defrosted and cooked in boiling salted water for 2 minutes) or use fresh peas from the pod
Sea salt and freshly ground black pepper

There isn't a lot of hunting to do here, but it's a must if you can to go picking wild garlic when it is in season. It's so pungent and fragrant and adds a distinctive flavour to the dish. You could use spinach instead of wild garlic. The garlic or spinach is teamed with cooked garlic bulbs here, which can easily be done in the slow cooker the day before, slowly steamed while wrapped in foil.

1. To steam the garlic in the slow cooker, rub each garlic bulb with olive oil, then wrap them individually in foil. Sit them in the slow cooker, put the lid on and cook on Low for 4 hours. Remove carefully using tongs as they will be hot! Put to one side until ready to use.

2. For the rice, heat the olive oil in a frying pan, add the onion, season well and cook for a couple of minutes. Stir in the celery and cook for a few minutes more. Tip this into the slow cooker along with the rice, butter and stock. Put the lid on and cook for 2½ hours on High.

3. Stir through the wild garlic leaves or wilted spinach and the peas, then top with the whole garlic bulbs and wild garlic flowers, if using. To eat, you can squeeze as much garlic out of the cloves as you wish and stir it through the rice.

Spring carrot and chives soup

SERVES 4–6
PREP 10 MINS
COOK 8 HOURS ON LOW

½ tbsp olive oil
1 onion, roughly chopped
3 cloves garlic, roughly chopped
2 medium potatoes, peeled and roughly chopped
800g spring carrots, roughly chopped
Bunch of chives, roughly chopped, reserve some for garnish
900ml hot vegetable stock
Sea salt and freshly ground black pepper

It's so easy to make the perfect soup in the slow cooker – just set the timer then blitz. This is a really simply flavoured soup, but it's easily jazzed up with ginger, coriander, curry powder or fresh chillies, if preferred.

1. Add all the ingredients to the slow cooker, put the lid on and set for 8 hours on Low.

2. Blitz with a stick blender – if it is too thick, add a little hot water from the kettle. Alternatively, add it all to a blender and blitz. Taste and season some more, if needed. Garnish with the chives and serve with crusty rolls.

Braised leeks, courgettes, spring carrots and tarragon with a mustard dressing

SERVES 4
PREP 15 MINS
COOK 3–3½ HOURS ON HIGH

- 2 tbsp olive oil
- 3 leeks, trimmed, washed and cut into 3 chunky pieces
- 3 courgettes, trimmed and cut into chunky pieces
- 200g spring carrots or carrots cut into fine lengths
- A few tarragon leaves, plus extra for garnish (or use thyme)
- 50g butter (optional)
- 200ml hot vegetable stock (for oven method)
- 4 strips of lemon zest
- Sea salt and freshly ground black pepper
- Thyme leaves, for garnish (optional)

For the dressing
- 6 tbsp extra virgin olive oil
- 2 tbsp white wine vinegar
- 2 tsp Dijon mustard
- Pinch of sugar

These few simple ingredients result in a stunning dish. Use all baby vegetable versions if available, although cooking times may need to be reduced slightly. Serve as a side dish or a main with new potatoes and salad.

1. Drizzle half the olive oil into the slow cooker, then add the leek, courgette and carrots. Top with the tarragon and butter, if using, and season well. Add the lemon zest strips and drizzle over the remaining oil. Put the lid on and set for 3–3½ hours on High. Poke the vegetables to check if they are tender.

2. To make the dressing, whisk together the olive oil and vinegar, then whisk in the mustard and sugar until they emulsify, and season well.

3. To serve, drizzle the dressing over the warm vegetables and garnish with fresh thyme or tarragon or both.

Spring veg katsu curry

SERVES 4
PREP 20 MINS
COOK SAUCE 3 HOURS ON HIGH/VEGETABLES 2½ HOURS ON HIGH

For the curry sauce
½ tsp olive oil
1 onion, roughly chopped
3 cloves garlic, roughly chopped
5cm piece of fresh ginger, peeled and chopped
1 red chilli, deseeded and chopped
3 carrots, sliced
1 crisp apple, chopped
3 tbsp medium curry powder
1 tsp ground turmeric
1 tsp ground cumin
1 tsp ground fenugreek
1 tsp ground coriander
2 tbsp dark soy sauce
2 tbsp maple syrup
1 tbsp rice wine vinegar
2 tsp white miso (sweet)
300ml hot vegetable stock
Sea salt and freshly ground black pepper

For the vegetables
2 tbsp plain flour
2 eggs, lightly beaten
400g panko breadcrumbs
2 tbsp olive oil (extra needed for hob method)
200g Tenderstem broccoli, trimmed and halved lengthways
3 chunky courgettes, trimmed and sliced on the diagonal
Bunch of spring onions, trimmed, white part left whole, green part chopped, for garnish

This is a two-part recipe and it's best to make the sauce ahead, then you can cook the vegetables when you're ready to serve. The curry sauce is deliciously sweet and reminiscent of chip-shop curry sauce. It makes the perfect combo with the breaded vegetables, but there are no rules to say you can't have it with chips too!

1. To make the sauce, add all the ingredients into the slow cooker. Give them a stir, put the lid on and set on High for 3 hours. Blitz with a stick blender until smooth or transfer to a blender, then taste and season as needed.

2. To make the vegetables, place the flour, egg and breadcrumbs on separate plates. Drizzle the olive oil into the slow cooker. Toss the vegetables in the flour, then egg, then coat in the breadcrumbs and layer in the slow cooker. Sit the lid on and cook on High for 2½ hours. Halfway through, flip the vegetables using a fish slice so the cooked ones are now on top.

3. Serve the sauce, piping hot, with the vegetables, and scatter over the chopped green spring onions.

LIGHT & BRIGHT

Veggie sausage and beans in spicy tomato sauce with baked eggs, feta and coriander

SERVES 4
PREP 10 MINS
COOK 9 HOURS ON LOW

1 tbsp olive oil
1 onion, finely chopped
3 cloves garlic, finely chopped
250g dried haricot beans, pinto beans or cannellini beans, rinsed
1 tbsp tamarind pulp or use 1 tbsp tamarind paste
300ml hot vegetable stock
1 tsp English mustard
2 tsp smoked paprika
2 x 400g tins of chopped tomatoes
1 tbsp maple syrup
Pinch of chilli flakes
8 vegetarian sausages
4 eggs
Sea salt and freshly ground black pepper
150g feta, crumbled, for garnish
Handful of coriander leaves, for garnish

Dried haricot and pinto beans just work so well in the slow cooker! It makes using them a breeze – no soaking and no worrying whether they are fully cooked. You will need to soak dried cannellini beans overnight if you decide to use them. This is posh baked beans. The tamarind adds a subtle acidic accent to the dish, while the eggs and tangy feta make for a mouthwatering combo.

1. Heat the oil in a frying pan, add the onion and season well, then cook for a couple of minutes. Stir in the garlic and add the mixture to the slow cooker along with the beans.

2. In a jug, mix the tamarind pulp, if using, with the hot stock, stir until dissolved, then pour it into the pot. If using the paste, just stir this in and add the stock. Stir in the mustard, paprika, tomatoes, maple syrup and chilli flakes. Put the lid on and cook for 9 hours on Low or until the beans are fully cooked and tender. If it looks overly dry, top up with a little hot water from the kettle.

3. Add the sausages for the last hour of cooking. Then, for the last 15 minutes of cooking, make four indents in the sauce and crack an egg into each. Put the lid on until they are cooked. Scatter over the feta and coriander and serve.

Courgette, pea, red pepper and goat's cheese frittata

SERVES 4
PREP 15 MINS
COOK 2–2½ HOURS ON HIGH

1 tbsp olive oil
1 red onion, finely chopped
3 cloves garlic, finely chopped
2 courgettes, trimmed and sliced
2 red peppers, deseeded and chopped into bite-sized pieces
6 large eggs
200g frozen peas (defrosted) or use fresh peas from the pod
120g goat's cheese, crumbled
½ bunch of chives, finely chopped
½ bunch of mint, chopped
Sea salt and freshly ground black pepper

This is a fresh mix of colourful veg, lightly cooked in eggs, which makes a good family-sized frittata or keep in the fridge and serve in slices as required if feeding fewer. It only requires a salad of some description and some good bread.

1. Heat the oil in a large frying pan, add the onion, season well and cook for a couple of minutes, then stir in the garlic and cook for a minute more. Add the courgette and peppers and toss around the pan for a minute so they get well coated with the oil, then transfer the mixture into the slow cooker.

2. Put the lid on and cook for 1 hour on High, then mix the eggs, peas, goat's cheese, chives and mint, pour them over the vegetables and turn to coat.

3. Now set the slow cooker for a further 1 hour or until the eggs are just set – they will continue to cook a little longer in the residue heat. The frittata may need a little longer, but be careful of the eggs overcooking and scrambling. Let it sit for 5 minutes, then slice and serve.

Red Thai tofu curry

SERVES 4
PREP 20 MINS
COOK 4 HOURS ON HIGH

1 tbsp olive oil
4 shallots, finely chopped
3 cloves garlic, finely chopped
5cm piece of fresh ginger, peeled and grated
1 red chilli, deseeded and finely chopped (or use more for heat)
1 lemongrass, trimmed and grated (a microplane works best)
1–2 tsp gochujang chilli paste (or use more for heat)
2 tbsp tomato purée
3 tbsp dark soy sauce
Juice of 2 limes
1 tbsp demerara sugar
1 tsp ground coriander
1 tsp ground cumin
Handful of Thai basil leaves, torn, reserve some for garnish
300g cherry tomatoes
200ml hot vegetable stock
400ml tin of coconut milk (use full-fat version to prevent splitting)
130g baby sweetcorn
150g sugar snap peas
2–3 tbsp vegetable oil
396g pack of firm tofu, cut into cubes
220g baby spinach leaves
Sea salt and freshly ground black pepper
Coriander leaves, for garnish

This recipe uses Thai red curry paste made from scratch, similar to the paste used in the Thai green curry on page 25. It may taste slightly different to the ready-bought paste, but it's much tastier and you know exactly what you are putting into your pot. You can easily raise the heat with the addition of more chillies.

1. Heat the olive oil in a large frying pan, add the shallots, season well and cook for a couple of minutes, then stir in the garlic, ginger, chilli and lemongrass and cook for a couple of minutes more. Transfer the mixture to the slow cooker.

2. To the slow cooker add the gochujang paste, tomato purée, soy sauce, lime juice, sugar, spices, Thai basil leaves, cherry tomatoes and stock. Stir well, put the lid on and set the cooker for 4 hours on High.

3. For the last hour, tip in the coconut milk, baby sweetcorn and sugar snap peas.

4. To cook the tofu, heat 1 tablespoon of the vegetable oil in the frying pan, add the tofu (you may have to do this in batches) and cook for several minutes, turning occasionally until golden. Top up with more oil as needed. Stir the spinach into the curry and, once wilted, stir in the tofu. Garnish with coriander and Thai basil leaves.

2.
Fresh & Fragrant

Smoky peppers and potatoes with toasted almonds

SERVES 4
PREP 15 MINS
COOK 3 HOURS ON HIGH

1 tbsp olive oil, plus an extra splash
1 red onion, roughly chopped
4 cloves garlic, finely sliced
A few thyme sprigs, plus extra for garnish
4–5 medium waxy potatoes, peeled and chopped into wedges
2–3 tsp sweet smoked paprika
4 mixed peppers (red and yellow), deseeded and quartered
8 sweet mini peppers, left whole
Sea salt and freshly ground black pepper
Handful of skinned almonds, lightly toasted, for garnish
150g feta cheese, crumbled, for garnish

Peppers cook so well in the slow cooker. They just require a little oil for the flavour to be really released. The small peppers are thrown in whole, so may need a little pulling apart when serving. A salad on the side, some French bread, feta strewn on top and a jug of rosé . . . you've got summer on the table!

1. Heat the olive oil in a frying pan, add the onion, season well and cook for a couple of minutes, then add the garlic, thyme, potatoes and paprika and cook, stirring, for a further minute or two.

2. Add the contents of the pan to the slow cooker along with both types of peppers and a further splash of olive oil, season again, give it a stir, cover with the lid and cook on High for 3 hours.

3. When ready to serve, toast the almonds in a frying pan until pale golden, then roughly chop. Scatter the almonds, feta and thyme over the peppers. Serve with French bread.

Slow-cooked cherry tomatoes with garlic

SERVES 4
PREP 5 MINS
COOK 3 HOURS ON HIGH

1 tbsp olive oil (extra needed for oven method)
1kg cherry tomatoes, rinsed
1 garlic bulb, separated and peeled
Sea salt and freshly ground black pepper
Large handful of basil leaves, torn, plus extra leaves for garnish

This is the sauce for long summer days when tomatoes are in abundance and rich in sunshine nutrients. Cherry tomato skins are easier to eat, but use regular tomatoes, halved, if you have a glut of them. Serve this as a side vegetable, warm or at room temperature, or toss with linguine and top with lots of fresh basil.

1. Splash half the olive oil into the slow cooker, then add the tomatoes and garlic and season really well.

2. Drizzle over the remaining olive oil, put the lid on and cook on High for 3 hours.

3. Squash a few of the tomatoes and stir in the torn basil, then garnish with the whole basil leaves. Serve as a vegetable on the side or tossed through pasta, or it's delicious used to top some sourdough toast.

Chunky Spanish stew

SERVES 4–6
PREP 20 MINS
COOK 5 HOURS ON HIGH

1 tbsp olive oil
1 large onion, halved and fairly thickly sliced
3 cloves garlic, finely sliced
Pinch of saffron
2 tsp smoked paprika
1 tsp paprika
2 tbsp dry sherry (check it is vegetarian)
2 tsp sherry vinegar
4 mixed peppers (red and green), deseeded and roughly chopped
2kg potatoes, peeled and roughly chopped
Handful of thyme leaves, chopped, plus a few extra for garnish
500ml passata
300ml hot vegetable stock
Handful of sultanas
Handful of pine nuts, plus a few extra (toast these in a frying pan) for garnish
Sea salt and freshly ground black pepper

This is a burst of summer flavours, perfect to have ready for some alfresco eating. It is packed with the heady spices of smoked paprika and saffron, which perfectly complement the pine nuts and sultanas in a rich tomato base.

1. Heat the olive oil in a frying pan, add the onion, season well and cook for a couple of minutes, then add the garlic and cook for a minute more. Stir in the spices, sherry and vinegar, raise the heat and let it bubble for a couple of minutes to allow the alcohol to evaporate, then transfer it all to the slow cooker.

2. Now add in the peppers, potatoes and thyme, give it a stir and then add the passata, stock, sultanas and pine nuts. Stir again, put the lid on and set on High for 5 hours.

3. To serve, top with the toasted pine nuts and extra thyme leaves and serve with crusty bread to mop up the juices.

Aubergine makhani

SERVES 4
PREP 10 MINS
COOK 5 HOURS ON HIGH

1 tbsp olive oil
1 onion, finely chopped
4 cloves garlic, finely chopped
1 red chilli, deseeded and finely chopped (add more if you like more heat)
5cm piece of fresh ginger, peeled and finely chopped
2 tsp garam masala
6 cardamom pods, crushed and seeds removed
1 tsp ground coriander
1 tsp dried curry leaves, crushed
50g butter
2 large aubergines, cut into cubes
50g ground almonds
2 x 400g tins of chopped tomatoes
300ml water
2 tbsp double cream (optional)
Bunch of coriander leaves, chopped, reserve a few for garnish
Sea salt and freshly ground black pepper

Not a hot curry, but one packed with flavour and creamy deliciousness from the ground almonds and a little butter that simmer away slowly in the sauce. Aubergines are great for the slow cooker because they retain their shape and richness of flavour. Stirring through a little cream at the end of cooking is down to preference or if you have some in the fridge – it is good with or without it.

1. Heat the oil in a frying pan, add the onion, season well and cook for a couple of minutes. Stir in the garlic, chilli and ginger and then add the garam masala, cardamom seeds, ground coriander and curry leaves and cook for a further minute.

2. Tip it all into the slow cooker along with the butter, aubergine, ground almonds, tomatoes and water. Stir again so the aubergine gets nicely coated, put the lid on and cook on High for 5 hours. Stir in the cream for the last 15 minutes of cooking, if using. If it is too thick, you can add a little hot water from the kettle to loosen it a little.

3. Check the seasoning, stir through the coriander and garnish with coriander leaves. Serve with rice and a spoon of mango chutney on the side or hot pickle chutney.

Courgette and tomato Provençal tian topped with goat's cheese

SERVES 4
PREP 25 MINS
COOK 3 HOURS ON HIGH

1 tbsp olive oil, plus extra for drizzling
2 red onions, halved then sliced
3 cloves garlic, finely sliced
3 courgettes, trimmed and sliced
6 tomatoes, sliced
4–6 medium potatoes, sliced into discs
Pinch of sumac
Pinch of dried oregano
A few thyme leaves, plus stems for garnish
100g goat's cheese, crumbled or sliced
Drizzle of balsamic vinegar (optional)
Sea salt and freshly ground black pepper

This really is summer in a pot and it looks rather more elaborate than it actually is. Goat's cheese makes a great tangy topping, plus it adds some protein to the dish. This would also be delicious served with hard-boiled eggs.

1. Heat the olive oil in a frying pan, add the onion, season well and cook for a few minutes, then add the garlic and cook for a few minutes more.

2. Drizzle a little oil in the slow cooker, then arrange the courgettes, tomatoes and potatoes in the slow cooker sat on their side. Layer them with the onion mixture, a pinch of sumac, oregano and thyme leaves. Drizzle over a little more olive oil and season again. Put the lid on and cook on High for 3 hours or until the potatoes are tender.

3. Top with the goat's cheese and allow it to melt. Garnish with fresh thyme and a drizzle of balsamic vinegar, if using. Serve with a rocket salad.

Slow-cooked BBQ jackfruit with slaw

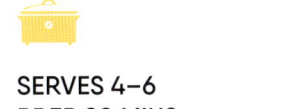

SERVES 4–6
PREP 20 MINS
COOK 6 HOURS ON HIGH

1 tbsp olive oil
2 red onions, finely chopped
3 cloves garlic, finely chopped
600ml passata
2 tbsp tomato ketchup
200ml cider or white wine vinegar
3 tbsp demerara sugar
Pinch of chilli flakes
1 tbsp soy sauce
2 tsp paprika
1 tsp English mustard

2 x 400g tins of jackfruit, drained and rinsed
Sea salt and freshly ground black pepper

For the slaw
½ large white cabbage, trimmed and finely shredded
3 medium carrots, peeled with a T-peeler
Good dollop of mayonnaise
1 tsp Dijon mustard

This is a great make-ahead dish as the flavours just get better as it sits a while. It's also a good one to have at the ready for a BBQ. Serve with warmed flatbreads and a dollop of this simple slaw.

1. Heat the olive oil in a frying pan, add the onion, season well and cook for a couple of minutes. Stir through the garlic and cook for a minute more. Transfer it all to the slow cooker.

2. Now add the passata, tomato ketchup, vinegar, sugar, chilli flakes, soy sauce, paprika and mustard. Tip in the jackfruit, give it a stir, put the lid on and cook on High for 6 hours.

3. To make the slaw, add the cabbage and carrot to a bowl, season and mix in the mayo and mustard to coat.

4. To serve, pull the jackfruit chunks apart using two forks to shred it and stir it through the sauce. Serve the sauce with warmed flatbreads and the slaw.

Aubergine and tomato stew

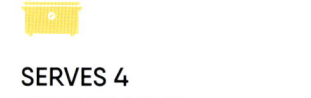

SERVES 4
PREP 20 MINS
COOK 6 HOURS ON HIGH

3 tbsp olive oil
1 red onion, finely chopped
2 sticks celery, finely chopped
3 cloves garlic, finely chopped
1 tsp dried oregano
1 tsp fennel seeds
4 aubergines, quartered lengthways, then sliced
500g cherry tomatoes
1 tsp white miso (sweet) mixed with 100ml hot water
Handful of pitted green olives (or use black if you prefer)
Sea salt and freshly ground black pepper
Handful of flat-leaf parsley, chopped, for garnish
Handful of basil leaves, for garnish

I've called this a stew, but it's similar to a caponata, minus the vinegar, which makes it a really versatile dish. It can be served hot with grains, toasted ciabatta and any leftovers or served at room temperature with a salad. However it is served, it makes a tasty, bold dish for when aubergines are in season. It would also be delicious topped with the sweet onions recipe on page 21.

1. Heat 1 tablespoon of the olive oil in a frying pan, add the onion and celery, season well and cook for a couple of minutes. Add the garlic, oregano and fennel seeds and cook for a minute more.

2. Transfer the mixture to the slow cooker along with the aubergine and cherry tomatoes. Pour over the miso stock, add the remaining oil, stir and sit the lid on top. Cook on High for 6 hours.

3. Throw the olives in for the last hour of cooking. Taste and season some more if needed. Garnish with the chopped parsley and basil leaves. Serve with brown rice or bulgur wheat and some toasted ciabatta.

Vietnamese tofu pot with basil and mint

SERVES 4
PREP 20 MINS
COOK 5 HOURS ON HIGH

1 tbsp olive oil
10 shallots, peeled and left whole
3 cloves garlic, finely sliced
1 tsp coriander seeds
2 star anise
4 carrots, cut into batons
5cm piece of fresh ginger, peeled and finely sliced
1 red chilli, finely sliced, plus 1 red chilli, sliced into rings, for garnish
1 lemongrass, trimmed and finely sliced
150g shiitake mushrooms, left whole
700ml hot mushroom or vegetable stock
200g sugar snap peas, finely sliced
2–3 tbsp vegetable oil
369g pack of firm tofu, sliced into chunky pieces
Handful of fresh herbs (Thai basil, mint, coriander), for garnish
Lime wedges (optional), for garnish
Splash of dark soy sauce (for hob method)
Sea salt and freshly ground black pepper

This is all about the broth – light and fragrant and topped with lots of fresh herbs. Make it as hot as you like. It feels restorative, revitalising and nutritious, bursting with colour and texture. The tofu is cooked separately to avoid it becoming soggy and is added at the end. You could easily do this ahead and refrigerate until ready to use.

1. Heat the olive oil in a frying pan, add the shallots, season well and cook for a few minutes until the shallots start to colour a little. Add the garlic, coriander seeds and star anise and cook for a further minute. Transfer it all into the slow cooker.

2. Now add the carrot, ginger, chilli, lemongrass and mushrooms, pour over the stock, put the lid on and cook on High for 5 hours.

3. Add the sugar snap peas for the last 15 minutes of cooking.

4. To prepare the tofu, heat a little of the vegetable oil in a large non-stick frying pan or wok and add the tofu. You may need to do this in batches as you don't want to overcrowd the pan. Cook until golden on both sides, topping up with more oil as you need it. Drain on a plate lined with kitchen paper to remove any excess oil.

5. Add the tofu to the pot for serving, then top with fresh herbs and garnish with sliced chilli and lime wedges, if using.

Caribbean sunshine stew with mango

SERVES 4
PREP 20 MINS
COOK 4 HOURS ON HIGH

- 1 tbsp olive oil
- 1 onion, finely chopped
- 3 cloves garlic, finely sliced
- 1 tsp each of cumin seeds, coriander seeds, mustard seeds and whole allspice (crushed in a pestle and mortar)
- 1 tsp ground ginger
- 1 tsp ground turmeric
- 6 tomatoes, roughly chopped
- 3 mixed peppers (red, yellow and orange), deseeded and roughly chopped
- 2 sweet potatoes, peeled and cut into bite-sized pieces
- 1–2 red or green chillies, deseeded and finely sliced, or use 2–3 fine slices from a Scotch bonnet chilli (note: these are very fiery hot chillies)
- 400g tin of black-eyed beans, drained and rinsed
- Handful of thyme leaves, reserve some for garnish
- Handful of dried mango pieces
- 500ml hot vegetable stock
- Sea salt and freshly ground black pepper
- Fresh mango pieces, to serve

Hot or not, that's up to you – use regular chilli or a Scotch bonnet for more heat. This is full of sunshine veg as the title suggests and double mango, dried and fresh, adds a delicious sweet tang to the flavour.

1. Heat the oil in a frying pan, add the onion and season well. Cook for a couple of minutes, then stir in the garlic and all the spices and cook for a further minute. Transfer it all to the slow cooker.

2. To the slow cooker, now add the tomatoes, peppers, sweet potato, chilli, beans, thyme leaves and dried mango pieces, giving them a bit of a stir to combine.

3. Pour over the hot stock, then put the lid on and cook for 4 hours on High.

4. Serve the stew on its own or with rice, topped with thyme leaves and fresh mango pieces.

Summer vegetables *au vin* topped with gherkins

SERVES 4
PREP 20 MINS
COOK 2½–3 HOURS ON HIGH

1 tbsp olive oil
1 onion, finely chopped
3 cloves garlic, finely chopped
1 large glass of white wine
Handful of thyme leaves, reserve some for garnish
2 leeks, trimmed, washed and cut into chunky pieces
180g stringless beans, sliced
3 courgettes, trimmed, sliced lengthways and cut into chunky pieces
2 tsp English mustard
500ml hot vegetable stock
4 tbsp double cream
250g spinach leaves
Sea salt and freshly ground black pepper
Cornichons (baby gherkins), to serve

The vegetables are simmered in stock and wine with added cream – this demands some rustic bread for juice mopping! Simple flavours for an easy, sophisticated dish.

1. Heat the oil in a large frying pan, add the onion, season well and cook for a couple of minutes, then stir through the garlic and add the wine. Turn the heat up and let it bubble for a few minutes. You need to do this step before adding it to the slow cooker. It will intensify the overall taste of the dish as the alcohol will evaporate but leave the flavour behind. Transfer it to the slow cooker.

2. Add the thyme, leeks, beans, courgettes and mustard and stir, then pour over the hot stock. Put the lid on and cook for 2½–3 hours on High.

3. For the last 15 minutes, stir in the double cream. When the dish is ready, stir in the spinach. Taste and season some more as needed. Serve topped with cornichons and bread on the side.

Stuffed aubergines with fresh tomato and parsley

SERVES 4
PREP 15 MINS
COOK 5 HOURS ON HIGH

3–4 tbsp olive oil
1 onion, finely chopped
4 cloves garlic, finely chopped
1 red chilli, deseeded and finely chopped
4 aubergines, sat upright, top sliced off, flesh removed and reserved (slice horizontal for oven method)
2–3 tomatoes, finely chopped
Juice of 1 lemon
400g tin of chickpeas, drained and rinsed
Bunch of flat-leaf parsley, chopped
Sea salt and freshly ground black pepper
Drizzle of pomegranate molasses, to serve (optional)
Baguette, sliced, toasted and rubbed with a garlic clove and drizzle of olive oil, to serve

This is the perfect make-ahead as you can serve it hot or cold. The aubergines are unconventionally stuffed upright – this is just so four aubergines will fit into the slow-cooker pot. Serve with toasted baguette and a lightly dressed green salad.

1. Heat 1 tablespoon of oil in a large frying pan, add the onion, season well and cook for a couple of minutes, then stir through the garlic and chilli and cook for a minute more. Add the aubergine flesh, tomato and lemon juice and cook for 5 minutes, chopping it a little with the side of a wooden spoon. Stir in the chickpeas and parsley.

2. Drizzle 1 tablespoon of oil in the bottom of the slow cooker and smother the hollowed-out aubergines with a little oil to coat inside and out. Now divide the mixture up among the aubergines and sit them upright in the slow cooker. If there is any extra mixture, it can just be added to the pot. One last drizzle of olive oil, then put the lid on and set on High for 5 hours.

3. When ready, drizzle with pomegranate molasses, if using, and slice the aubergines in half to serve. Serve with toasted baguette and salad.

Korean spicy sauce with pak choi and noodles

SERVES 4
PREP 15 MINS
COOK 4½ HOURS
ON HIGH

Bunch of spring onions, trimmed, white part finely chopped
3 cloves garlic, finely sliced
5cm piece of fresh ginger, peeled and finely sliced
2 sticks celery, diced
250g cherry tomatoes
Bunch of coriander, finely chopped
1 tbsp sesame oil
1 tbsp red wine vinegar
1 tbsp demerara sugar
2 tbsp dark soy sauce
2 tsp gochujang chilli paste (or more if you like it hot – different brands have different levels of heat)
300ml mushroom or vegetable stock
250g pak choi, base trimmed and leaves separated
500g ready-to-wok udon thick or medium noodles or noodles of your choice
Sea salt and freshly ground black pepper
Handful of sesame seeds, for garnish

Hot and spicy with a hint of sweetness. You can get hold of gochujang paste from most large supermarkets or Asian stores. It's a good store-cupboard staple to have in for Korean-inspired dishes. Udon noodles have been tossed with the sauce here as they offer the perfect 'slurp', but do choose a more authentic noodle or just use your favourite ones.

1 Add all the ingredients to the slow cooker except the pak choi, noodles and sesame seeds. Season well, give it a stir, put the lid on and cook for 4½ hours on High.

2 Add the pak choi for the last 15 minutes of cooking, then stir through the noodles to warm through.

3 Sprinkle with sesame seeds to serve.

Indonesian-style summer rice pot

SERVES 6–8
PREP 15 MINS
COOK 2½ HOURS
ON HIGH

Splash of sesame oil
1 red onion, diced
3 cloves garlic, finely chopped
5cm piece of fresh ginger, peeled and finely chopped
1 green chilli, deseeded and finely chopped
2 tbsp kecap manis (sweet soy sauce)
1 tbsp dark soy sauce
2 tsp demerara sugar
Juice of 1 lime
1 tbsp rice wine vinegar
1 courgette, trimmed and diced
1 yellow and 1 red pepper, halved, deseeded and diced
165g tin of sweetcorn (drained weight)
300g basmati rice
700ml hot vegetable stock
Sea salt and freshly ground black pepper

For the topping
400g pineapple, finely chopped
2–3 tomatoes, finely chopped
Handful of salted peanuts, finely chopped
Fried egg per person (optional)

Rice and spice are always a winner at any time of the day and this is packed with colourful vegetables simmered in a rich and sweet soy sauce. Adorn it as you wish: chopped peanuts, pineapple and tomato all zip through the richness, while a fried egg on top turns it into something utterly delicious.

1. Heat the sesame oil in a frying pan, add the onion, season well and cook for a couple of minutes, then stir in the garlic, ginger and chilli and cook for a couple of minutes more. Transfer the mixture to the slow cooker.

2. Stir in the remaining ingredients, put the lid on and set on High for 2½ hours. Stir and check the rice is cooked.

3. Stir through most of the pineapple and scatter the rest on top, along with the tomato and peanuts. Serve with a fried egg on top, if you wish.

Superfood rice, grain and bean pot with nori seaweed and avocado

SERVES 4–6
PREP 5 MINS
COOK 2–2½ HOURS ON HIGH

1 tbsp olive oil
Bunch of spring onions, trimmed, white part finely chopped, green parts reserved for garnish
3 cloves garlic, finely chopped
5cm piece of fresh ginger, peeled and grated
400g white basmati rice or use brown (add a little more water for brown and it will need the full 2½ hours)
700ml hot vegetable stock
100g flaxseeds (brown linseed)
400g tin of chickpeas, drained and rinsed
3 sheets of nori seaweed, finely chopped, crumbled or blitzed in a blender (mix it with a little sea salt before adding)
Pinch of chilli flakes (optional)
Sea salt and freshly ground black pepper
2 avocados, halved, stoned and sliced, for garnish
Handful of pumpkin seeds, for garnish
Lime wedges, to serve

You can serve this on its own or it's a great rice recipe to make and have stored in the fridge to eat as an accompaniment to dishes. You can get creative with the toppings: watercress, orange segments, pomegranate seeds and baby tomatoes would all be a tasty addition.

1. Heat the olive oil in a frying pan, add the spring onion, season well and cook for a couple of minutes, then stir in the garlic and ginger and cook for a minute more. Transfer it to the slow cooker.

2. Stir in the rice so it is all coated, then pour in the stock, add the flaxseeds and chickpeas, stir, put the lid on and set on High for 2–2½ hours, or until the rice is cooked. If it looks overly dry, top up with a little hot water from the kettle.

3. Stir through the seaweed and sea salt mix and add chilli flakes, if using. Top with avocado and pumpkin seeds to serve and squeeze over some fresh lime.

Butter beans in harissa and tahini sauce with dill and preserved lemon

SERVES 4
PREP 10 MINS
COOK 8 HOURS ON LOW

- 1 tbsp olive oil
- 1 onion, finely chopped
- 3 cloves garlic, sliced
- 2 tsp sumac
- 2 tsp dried mint
- 200g dried butter beans, regular or giant, rinsed
- 2 preserved lemons, pith removed and rind sliced
- 1 tbsp harissa
- 2 x 400g tins of chopped tomatoes
- Large handful of dill, chopped, reserve half for garnish
- 400ml water
- 2 tbsp tahini
- Sea salt and freshly ground black pepper
- Pomegranate seeds, to garnish (optional)
- Lemon wedges, to serve (optional)

Slow cookers are great for dried beans as they can simmer away for hours until tender, retain their shape and texture and don't require the pre-soaking. If you can get hold of giant butter beans, do use those, otherwise, use the regular size. The tahini is stirred through for the last half hour, just to prevent it from splitting. This dish can be served with bulgur wheat or couscous, both of which take only minutes to put together.

1. Heat the oil in a frying pan, add the onion, season well and cook, stirring, for a couple of minutes until softened, then stir in the garlic, sumac and mint and cook for a further minute.

2. Transfer the onion mix to the slow cooker along with the butter beans, preserved lemon, harissa, tomatoes, half the dill and the water. Put the lid on and cook on Low for 8 hours or until the beans are tender. If the mixture is becoming too dry, add a little hot water from the kettle. Stir through the tahini for the last 30 minutes.

3. Season to taste and top with the remaining dill and pomegranate seeds, if using. Serve with the lemon wedges, if using, and with bulgur wheat or couscous alongside.

Sweetcorn chowder

SERVES 4–6
PREP 20 MINS
COOK 4 HOURS ON HIGH

1 tbsp olive oil
Knob of butter
1 onion, finely chopped
3 cloves garlic, finely chopped
Pinch of ground cumin
2 medium potatoes, peeled and cubed
2 x 400g tins of sweetcorn, drained, or use
  4–5 corn on the cobs, kernels stripped
425g tin of creamed sweetcorn
200ml hot vegetable stock
200ml milk
200ml double cream, reserve a drizzle for serving
Sea salt and freshly ground black pepper
Watercress, for garnish

You could use fresh (if in season), frozen or tinned sweetcorn for this recipe, but it's the creamed sweetcorn that really makes it. To make it a more main meal soup, top it with chunky cheesy croutons. Here it is garnished simply with watercress, which adds a wonderful peppery hit.

1 Heat the olive oil and butter in a frying pan, add the onion, season well and cook for a couple of minutes, then stir through the garlic and cook for a minute more. Stir through the cumin.

2 Transfer to the slow cooker, stir in the potatoes and both kinds of sweetcorn, pour in the stock and set on High for 4 hours.

3 For the last hour, pour in the milk and cream. Blitz with a stick blender until almost smooth – it's nice to leave some texture – or transfer to a blender and blitz. Taste and season some more if needed. Serve with a drizzle of cream and garnish with watercress.

Greek-style stuffed peppers with rice and tomatoes

SERVES 4
PREP 10 MINS
COOK 6 HOURS ON HIGH

3 tbsp olive oil
4 large peppers (red and yellow), tops sliced off and reserved, deseeded and insides trimmed
1 red onion, finely chopped
3 cloves garlic, finely diced
2 tsp dried oregano
2 celery sticks, finely diced
Pinch of chilli flakes
150g white or brown basmati rice (brown rice will take longer to cook)
Pinch of sugar
500ml passata
Sea salt and freshly ground black pepper

These are a game-changer. Peppers in the slow cooker are cooked to perfection and, for ultimate ease, you can add uncooked rice to them with the safe knowledge that this will also be cooked to perfection. A really easy dish with stunning results.

1. Rub a little of the oil on the inside and outside of each pepper and drizzle 1 tablespoon of olive oil in the bottom of the slow cooker. Sit the peppers on their bases snugly in the slow cooker.

2. Heat the remaining oil in a frying pan (reserve a drizzle), add the onion and season well. Cook for a couple of minutes, then add the garlic and cook for a further minute. Now stir through the oregano, celery and chilli flakes and cook for a minute more. Stir through the rice, sugar and passata and stir until completely coated.

3. Divide the mixture into the peppers – they will be really full and it doesn't matter if some spills out. Put the tops on each, give it a final drizzle of olive oil and season again if you wish. Put the lid on and cook on High for 6 hours. Serve with a rocket and tomato salad.

Provençal green beans, olive and tomato

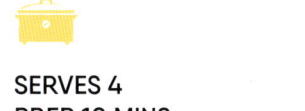

SERVES 4
PREP 10 MINS
COOK 3 HOURS ON HIGH

2 tbsp olive oil
1 red onion, roughly chopped
3 cloves garlic, finely sliced
1 tsp cumin seeds and 1 tsp coriander seeds
  (crushed in a pestle and mortar)
1 tsp ground cinnamon
1 tbsp red wine vinegar
450g green beans, trimmed and halved
300g cherry tomatoes
300g jar pitted black olives, drained
Sea salt and freshly ground black pepper

A pot of colour and freshness, this is just as good served hot or cold and as a main or side. Tangy olives make the perfect partner for green beans in this Provençal-style dish.

1. Heat half the olive oil in a frying pan, add the onion, season well and cook for a couple of minutes, then add the garlic and cook for a minute more. Stir in the spices and the red wine vinegar, let it bubble for a minute then transfer it all to the slow cooker.

2. Add the green beans, tomatoes and olives and drizzle over the remaining oil. Give it a stir, put the lid on and set on High for 3 hours. This would be great served with hard-boiled eggs or some Brie and crusty bread.

Sticky Japanese sauce with vegetables and noodles

SERVES 4
PREP 15 MINS, PLUS 30 MINS PICKLING
COOK 5 HOURS ON HIGH

For the sauce
3 cloves garlic, finely sliced
5cm piece of fresh ginger, peeled and finely sliced
Bunch of spring onions, trimmed, white part finely chopped, green part finely sliced, for garnish
3 tbsp maple syrup or runny honey
3 tbsp rice wine vinegar
1 tbsp black rice vinegar (optional)
2 tbsp hoisin sauce
1 tbsp light soy sauce
1 tbsp sriracha sauce
1 tsp Dijon mustard
Pinch of chilli flakes
Sea salt and freshly ground black pepper

For the pickled radish (optional, but tasty)
Small bunch of radishes, trimmed, washed and finely sliced
3 tbsp red wine vinegar
2–3 tbsp caster sugar

For the vegetables
1 tbsp sesame oil (for hob method)
300g baby sweetcorn, roughly sliced
1 head of broccoli, cut into tiny florets
220g green beans, trimmed and chopped into bite-sized pieces

180g vermicelli noodles (3 blocks)

A mix of mainly store-cupboard ingredients are simmered to make this fabulous sweet and sticky sauce. It's nice and rich to carry the delicate veg that are added at the end of cooking so they retain some 'bite'.

1. Add all the sauce ingredients to the slow cooker, put the lid on and set on High for 5 hours.

2. For the pickled radish, if making, put the radish in a bowl, mix the vinegar and sugar together, pour it over and stir well. Let it sit for at least 30 minutes before serving.

3. For the last hour of cooking, add the vegetables to the slow cooker, then, when ready, add the vermicelli bundles to the pot, pushing them down so they are under the sauce. You may have to do this a bit at a time as they soften into the sauce (adding them dry like this means they don't go soggy).

4. Leave the slow cooker on Warm until the noodles are heated through and you are ready to serve, then toss the noodles and veg so it all gets coated. Top with the reserved spring onion green tops and pickled radish, if using.

Sweet pepper and pea paneer curry

SERVES 4–6
PREP 15 MINS
COOK 4 HOURS ON HIGH

1 tbsp olive oil
1 large onion, finely chopped
5 cloves garlic, finely chopped
1 green chilli, deseeded and finely chopped
3 red peppers and 3 green peppers, deseeded and roughly chopped
500ml hot vegetable stock mixed with 1 tbsp tomato purée and 2 tbsp mild curry powder
500g paneer, cubed
200g frozen peas (defrosted)
Bunch of coriander leaves, chopped
Sea salt and freshly ground black pepper

Paneer and peppers are a great combination – sweet and fresh, cooked in a light curry 'gravy'. The paneer is added straight to the pot, rather than pan-frying first, resulting in a soft and creamy texture. Serve with rice and warm naan bread for the perfect easy supper.

1. Heat the oil in a large frying pan, add the onion, season well and cook for a couple of minutes. Stir in the garlic and chilli and cook for a minute more. Transfer to the slow cooker.

2. Now add the peppers and pour in the stock mixture. Put the lid on and set on High for 4 hours.

3. Add the paneer for the last hour of cooking, stirring through the peas and coriander for serving. Taste and season some more if needed. Serve with rice and warm naan bread.

3.
Comforting & Earthy

Slow cooker perfect jacket spuds

MAKES 4
PREP 5 MINS
COOK 5–5½ HOURS
  ON HIGH

4 large baking potatoes
Olive oil, to smother the potatoes, plus an extra drizzle
Sea salt

Jacket potatoes cook really well in the slow cooker: perfectly tender, soft and fluffy. You can also cook them a day ahead and reheat them in the microwave when ready to serve if you have a stew sitting in the slow cooker!

1 Wash and scrub the potatoes well, then dry them thoroughly.

2 Prick them all over with a fork, then rub each one all over with olive oil and sprinkle with sea salt.

3 Drizzle a little oil in the slow cooker, wrap each potato individually in foil and put them in the slow cooker. Put the lid on and cook for 5 hours on High.

4 Carefully open the foil, it will be hot. Poke the potatoes with a sharp knife to check that they are cooked. If not, give them another ½ hour.

5 When ready, slice the tops, fill with butter and put the lid back on until the butter melts, then serve with your choice of filling. Good with Tempeh stew (see page 146) or Butter beans in harissa and tahini sauce (see page 86).

Miso ramen with mushrooms, pickled red cabbage and soy-soaked eggs

SERVES 4
PREP 20 MINS
COOK 4 HOURS ON HIGH

1 tbsp sesame oil (use 1 tbsp olive oil for oven method)
Bunch of spring onions, trimmed, white part finely sliced, green part finely sliced, for garnish
3 cloves garlic, finely sliced
5cm piece of fresh ginger, peeled and finely sliced
1 red chilli, deseeded and finely sliced
1 butternut squash, halved, peeled, deseeded and cut into bite-sized chunks
15g porcini mushrooms (soaked in hot water for 15 mins, drained and chopped)
3 heaped tbsp white miso (sweet)
2 tbsp dark soy sauce, plus an extra splash
1 tbsp mirin
600ml hot vegetable stock
500g ready-to-wok udon noodles (your preferred thickness)
Sea salt and freshly ground black pepper
Handful of coriander leaves, for garnish
Black sesame seeds, to serve (optional)
Sriracha sauce, to serve (optional)

For the soy eggs
2 eggs, soft-boiled
3 tbsp dark soy sauce

For the red cabbage
½ red cabbage, finely shredded
Generous splash of rice wine vinegar
1 tbsp caster sugar

A ramen dish is a wonderful thing all year round, but it's the ultimate cold-weather food – it soothes without being heavy and it really hits the spot.

1. First, prepare the eggs. Peel the soft-boiled eggs and sit them in a bowl, pour over soy sauce to cover and turn the eggs occasionally. Leave for a couple of hours or overnight in the fridge.

2. To prepare the cabbage ahead, mix it with the vinegar and sugar and put it to one side for it to soften and the flavours to develop.

3. Heat the oil in a frying pan, add the spring onion, season well and cook for a couple of minutes, then stir through the garlic, ginger and chilli and cook for a minute more. Transfer to the slow cooker.

4. Add the butternut squash, porcini mushrooms, miso, soy sauce and mirin and pour in the hot stock. Stir, put the lid on and set for 4 hours on High.

5. When ready, stir through the noodles and allow them to warm through. Taste and season as needed – it may need a further splash of soy sauce. Serve topped with red cabbage, coriander leaves, green spring onions, soy eggs (halved), a sprinkle of black sesame seeds, if using, and a drizzle of sriracha, if using.

COMFORTING & EARTHY

Pumpkin, chestnuts, green chilli and cinnamon stew

SERVES 4
PREP 15 MINS
COOK 5 HOURS ON HIGH

1 tbsp olive oil
1 red onion, finely chopped
3 cloves garlic, sliced
1 green chilli, deseeded and finely chopped
3 tsp ground cinnamon
180g whole cooked chestnuts
1 small pumpkin or a butternut squash, peeled, deseeded and cubed
2 sage leaves, chopped
1 bay leaf
Pinch of chilli flakes (optional)
100g pearl barley
500ml passata
500ml hot vegetable stock
Sea salt and freshly ground black pepper
Handful of chopped flat-leaf parsley, for garnish

A heady mix of sweet, spicy and earthy, the pearl barley adds a delicious texture to the pot. Butternut squash will work just as well as pumpkin if it's not the season for them.

1. Heat the oil in a frying pan, add the onion, season well and cook for a couple of minutes, then stir in the garlic and green chilli and cook for a further minute. Stir through the cinnamon.

2. Transfer the mixture to the slow cooker along with the chestnuts, pumpkin or squash, sage leaves, bay leaf and chilli flakes, if using.

3. Stir in the pearl barley and turn to coat, then stir through the passata and hot stock. Put the lid on and cook on High for 5 hours.

4. Garnish with parsley and serve while piping hot with crusty bread on the side to mop up the juices.

Marrow and jackfruit casserole with cider, baby onions and apple

SERVES 4–6
PREP 20 MINS
COOK 5 HOURS ON HIGH

1 tbsp olive oil
12 baby onions, peeled
3 cloves garlic, finely chopped
A few thyme leaves
Pinch of chilli flakes
Pinch of paprika
Pinch of dried oregano
1 marrow, halved, peeled, deseeded and chopped
200ml dry cider
2 apples, peeled, cored and chopped

400g tin of chopped tomatoes
200ml hot vegetable stock
250g jackfruit, drained and rinsed, pulled apart and sliced
Sea salt and freshly ground black pepper

For the topping (optional)
Splash of olive oil
Handful of breadcrumbs
Handful of parsley, finely chopped
Zest of 1 lemon

A 'meaty' pot of goodness – seasonal marrow loves tomatoey flavours and this is simmered with cider and apple for a delicious autumnal mix. Top with a handful of toasted breadcrumbs for some added texture.

1. Heat the olive oil in a large, deep-sided frying pan, add the baby onions, season well and cook for about 5 minutes until beginning to soften. Stir in the garlic, thyme leaves, chilli flakes, paprika and oregano. Cook for 1 minute, then add the marrow and cook for a minute more. Pour in the cider and let it bubble for a couple of minutes.

2. Transfer it all to the slow cooker, add the apple and pour in the tomatoes and hot stock. Put the lid on and set on High for 5 hours. Stir in the jackfruit for the last hour of cooking.

3. If making the topping, pour a splash of olive oil into a frying pan and cook the breadcrumbs, parsley and lemon zest until toasted and golden. Sprinkle over to serve.

4. Serve the casserole with brown rice (see page 14) or bulgur wheat and crusty bread to mop up the delicious sauce.

Lentil and garlic stew topped with chilli oil

SERVES 4–6
PREP 20 MINS
COOK 8 HOURS ON LOW

1 tbsp olive oil
2 red onions, finely chopped
4 sticks celery, finely chopped
3 medium carrots, finely chopped
6 cloves garlic, finely sliced
500ml passata
400g tin of chopped tomatoes
500ml hot vegetable stock
1 tsp Dijon mustard
500g dried green or brown lentils
180g cavolo nero or curly kale, any chunky stalks removed
Sea salt and freshly ground black pepper
Grated vegetarian Parmesan, to serve (optional)
Chilli oil or flakes, to serve

This Italian-inspired dish really is a pot of goodness with protein-rich lentils and vitamin-fuelled kale. It's exactly what you need when it's cold outside. The magic mix of onion, celery and carrots is again softened first in a frying pan, but this isn't essential, just my preference. You could just throw everything in the slow cooker, turn the dial and go.

1. Heat the olive oil in a frying pan, add the onion, celery and carrot and season well. Cook for about 5 minutes, until starting to soften, then stir through the garlic and cook for 1 minute more.

2. Transfer the contents of the pan to the slow cooker along with the passata, chopped tomatoes, stock, mustard and lentils, then stir to combine. Put the lid on and cook on Low for 8 hours.

3. For the last hour of cooking, add the cavolo nero or kale. If you need a little more liquid, you can add some hot water now. Taste and season some more if needed.

4. Top with grated Parmesan, if using, and a drizzle of chilli oil or chilli flakes before serving with warm crusty bread alongside.

Cauliflower cheese soup with pickled walnuts

SERVES 6
PREP 15 MINS
COOK 6 HOURS ON LOW

Drizzle of olive oil
1 cauliflower, cut into florets
1 onion, roughly chopped
3 cloves garlic, chopped
2 medium potatoes, peeled and roughly chopped
2 tsp Dijon mustard
Good grating of nutmeg
900ml hot vegetable stock
400g Cheddar cheese, grated (or use Stilton)
Sea salt and freshly ground black pepper
Handful of pickled walnuts, drained and finely sliced, for garnish (optional)

You can't beat a soup on a cold day. The cauliflower retains all its flavour cooked like this in the slow cooker. Stir the cheese in at the end for maximum intensity – Stilton would also be a great choice. Pickled walnuts aren't everyone's favourite, but trust me, they are a really tasty addition, but not essential at all.

1 Add the olive oil, cauliflower, onion, garlic, potato, mustard, nutmeg, seasoning and stock to the slow cooker. Put the lid on and set the timer on Low for 6 hours.

2 Once cooked, blitz with a stick blender until smooth, then stir in the cheese, reserving a little for the top, and allow it to melt. Top with the reserved cheese and the pickled walnuts, if using. Dig in while hot with some warm crusty bread on the side.

COMFORTING & EARTHY

Lentils and veggie sausages in romesco-style sauce

SERVES 4–6
PREP 20 MINS
COOK 6 HOURS ON HIGH

1 tbsp olive oil
2 onions, roughly chopped
3 cloves garlic, roughly chopped
5 red peppers, deseeded and roughly chopped
1 tbsp sherry vinegar
2 tsp smoked paprika
1 red chilli and 1 green chilli, deseeded and finely chopped
100g blanched almonds
300g lentilles vertes, rinsed
400ml hot vegetable stock
6–8 vegetarian sausages, left whole or chopped
Sea salt and freshly ground black pepper

Romesco sauce is a Spanish red pepper and almond sauce, which can be used as a dip, but here it makes a delicious base for the lentils. The sauce is made first and blitzed before the lentils are added. You could always remove a little of the sauce and reserve it to spread on toasted ciabatta.

1. Heat the oil in a large frying pan, add the onion and season well, then cook for a couple of minutes. Stir in the garlic and peppers and cook for a couple of minutes more.

2. Transfer it all to the slow cooker, then add the sherry vinegar, smoked paprika, chilli and almonds. Put the lid on and set on High for 6 hours.

3. After 1½ hours, blitz the sauce with a stick blender until smooth (alternatively, add it to a blender and blitz, then return it to the slow cooker).

4. Now stir in the lentils and stock and sit the lid back on. For the last hour of cooking, add the vegetarian sausages.

Moussaka

SERVES 4–6
PREP 20 MINS
COOK 6 HOURS ON HIGH

3 aubergines, cut into 5mm rounds
3 tbsp olive oil (extra needed for oven method)
1 onion, finely chopped
3 cloves garlic, finely chopped
2 tsp ground cinnamon
3 tsp dried oregano
Generous grating of nutmeg
300g dried green or brown lentils, rinsed
500ml passata
3 medium potatoes, peeled and finely sliced
Sea salt and freshly ground black pepper

For the topping
450g pot of 5% fat Greek yoghurt (don't use 0% fat as it may curdle)
2 eggs

This is pure comfort food, and it's one of those dishes that get better over time when reheated, so it's the perfect make-ahead recipe. It's a layer of aubergine and potato with a tomatoey lentil mix and, for ease, it's topped with a Greek yoghurt and egg mix rather than a béchamel sauce.

1. First, brush each aubergine slice with olive oil, add to a non-stick frying pan, a few at a time, and cook for a few seconds on each side. Remove and put to one side (you can skip this step if you prefer – it just gives the aubergine a little extra flavour).

2. Heat half the remaining olive oil in the frying pan, add the onion, season well and cook for a couple of minutes, then stir through the garlic and cook for a minute more. Stir through the cinnamon, half the oregano and the nutmeg, lentils and passata.

3. Drizzle the remaining oil in the bottom of the slow cooker, add a layer of potatoes, then layer up with the lentil mixture, aubergine and potato, ending with a layer of potato. Put the lid on and set on High for 6 hours.

4. For the last hour, mix together the Greek yoghurt, the remaining oregano and the eggs and pour the mixture evenly over the top potato layer. Put the lid back on and continue cooking for the final hour until set. Serve with lightly dressed rocket.

Chunky 'roots' soup

SERVES 4
PREP 20 MINS
COOK 6 HOURS ON LOW

1 tbsp olive oil
1 onion, finely chopped
3 cloves garlic, finely chopped
1 tbsp mild curry powder
1 bay leaf
3 sweet potatoes, peeled and cut into bite-sized pieces
300g carrots, roughly chopped
400g parsnips, peeled and roughly chopped
1 tbsp tomato purée
1 tsp English mustard
100g dried red lentils (this is for thickening)
800ml hot vegetable stock
400g tin of butter beans, drained and rinsed
Dollop of horseradish, to serve (optional)
Sea salt and freshly ground black pepper

This is a warming and comforting soup. The flavours of the vegetables really come to life – intense and sweet with a light curry-flavour broth. A dollop of hot horseradish to serve notches it up to the next level!

1. Heat the oil in a frying pan, add the onion, season well and cook for a couple of minutes. Add the garlic and cook for a minute more, then stir in the curry powder and bay leaf and transfer it all to the slow cooker.

2. Add the sweet potato, carrot, parsnip, tomato purée and mustard to the slow cooker, then stir in the lentils and hot stock. Put the lid on and set on Low for 6 hours.

3. When ready, stir through the butter beans and let them warm through, then serve topped with a dollop of hot horseradish and crusty bread.

Squash, mushroom and spinach lasagne

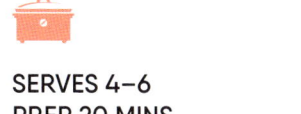

SERVES 4–6
PREP 20 MINS
COOK 5 HOURS ON HIGH

1 tbsp olive oil (extra needed for oven method)
1 onion, finely chopped
3 cloves garlic, finely chopped
1 tsp dried oregano
500ml passata
2 generous tsp vegetarian chilli pesto or sun-dried tomato pesto
1 small butternut squash, halved, peeled, deseeded and cut into small cubes
Pinch of chilli flakes (optional)
Pinch of grated nutmeg
250g spinach leaves, roughly chopped
250g mushrooms, sliced
250g ricotta, lightly whipped
125g mozzarella, grated
8–10 lasagne sheets
25g vegetarian Parmesan, grated
Sea salt and freshly ground black pepper

A slow cooker lasagne recipe is great to add to your repertoire as it can be quite laborious to make. Here it comes together in two simple stages: first the squash sauce is cooked, then it is layered with pasta, ricotta and mozzarella.

1. Heat the oil in a frying pan, add the onion, season well and cook for a minute, then stir in the garlic and oregano and cook for a minute more.

2. Transfer the contents of the pan to the slow cooker. Add the passata, pesto, butternut squash, chilli flakes, if using, and nutmeg and give it a good stir. Put the lid on and cook on High for 3 hours or until the squash is tender.

3. Stir in the spinach and mushrooms. Once the spinach has wilted, spoon the mixture out into a large bowl.

4. Now assemble the lasagne. Start with a layer of the squash and mushroom mixture, followed by the ricotta, mozzarella and then the lasagne sheets (you will have to break these up to fit), ending up with a layer of the squash mixture. Top with Parmesan.

5. Put the lid on, and cook on High for a further 2 hours or until the pasta is tender when poked with a sharp knife. Serve with a rocket salad.

COMFORTING & EARTHY

Chickpea balls in tomato sauce

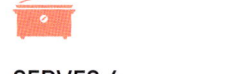

SERVES 4
PREP 20 MINS
COOK 4 HOURS ON HIGH

2 tbsp olive oil (extra needed for oven method)
2 onions, finely chopped
4 cloves garlic, finely chopped
2 sage leaves, finely chopped
400g tin of chickpeas, drained and rinsed
100g walnut halves
4 tbsp breadcrumbs
1 tsp dried oregano
1 tsp paprika

2 tsp white miso (sweet)
1 egg
Sea salt and freshly ground black pepper
Handful of flat-leaf parsley, chopped, for garnish

For the sauce
2 × 500ml passata
Pinch of chilli flakes
2 tsp capers, roughly chopped

These are so moreish – with walnut and miso in the mix, you get a good umami hit in every bite! The balls are cooked first and then topped with tomato sauce and cooked a little longer. Warning – they may fall apart slightly, but they are just as tasty!

1. Heat half the oil in a frying pan, add the onion, season well and cook for a minute, then add the garlic and sage leaves and cook for a minute more. Transfer half to a food processor (reserve half for the sauce) along with the chickpeas, walnut halves, breadcrumbs, oregano, paprika and miso and pulse until combined. Give it a taste before you combine with the egg, seasoning some more if needed. Then add the egg and pulse until it comes together. Roll into 16 balls.

2. Add the remaining olive oil to the slow cooker, then add the balls. Sit the lid on and cook on High for 4 hours. After 3 hours, carefully scoop them out and set aside.

3. Mix the reserved onion mixture with the passata, chilli flakes and capers, then tip this into the slow cooker. Add the balls back to the pot and into the sauce and cook for a further hour. Top with chopped parsley and serve with rice or spaghetti.

Black bean and squash stew with chipotle and sour cream drizzle

SERVES 6
PREP 15 MINS
COOK 6 HOURS ON HIGH

1 tbsp olive oil
1 onion, finely chopped
4 cloves garlic, finely chopped
1 green chilli, deseeded and finely chopped
1 tsp dried oregano
1 tsp ground cumin
1 tsp smoked paprika
1 small butternut squash, halved, peeled, deseeded and cut into small cubes
350g dried black turtle beans, rinsed
2 x 400g tins of chopped tomatoes + 1 empty tin of hot water
Juice of 1 lime
Bunch of coriander, leaves chopped, reserve a few leaves for garnish
Sea salt and freshly ground black pepper

For serving (pick and mix your favourites)
Chipotle sauce or Tabasco
Sour cream
½ red onion, finely sliced into rings (soaked in water for 5 mins and drained)
Lime wedges
2 avocados, halved, stoned, cubed and tossed in lime juice
Tortillas
Jalapeños

South American flavours get to mingle in the pot here. This recipe uses the meaty, smoky-flavoured black turtle beans, which are so called because of their little hard shells. Alternatively, you can use regular dried black beans.

1. Heat the oil in a frying pan, add the onion, season well and cook for a minute. Stir in the garlic and chilli and cook for a minute more. Stir through the spices and let them cook for a few seconds, then transfer everything to the slow cooker.

2. Add the squash, beans, tinned tomatoes and water and lime juice, stir and put the lid on. Cook on High for 6 hours or until the beans are tender.

3. Stir through most of the coriander. Top with a drizzle of chipotle sauce and sour cream and scatter over the remaining coriander leaves, red onion slices and lime wedges. Serve with avocado, tortillas and jalapeños.

COMFORTING & EARTHY

Persian-style veggie mince

SERVES 4
PREP 10 MINS
COOK 3 HOURS ON HIGH

1 tbsp olive oil
1 red onion, finely chopped
3 cloves garlic, finely chopped
1 tsp ground turmeric
1 tsp ground cumin
1 tsp ground cinnamon
2 tsp sumac
1 tsp pul biber (Aleppo pepper/Turkish chilli flakes) or use regular chilli flakes
454g pack (or similar weight) plant-based mince, defrosted if frozen

100g walnuts, roughly chopped
150g dried apricots, roughly chopped
1 tbsp tomato purée
600ml hot vegetable stock
Bunch of coriander, leaves chopped
Sea salt and freshly ground black pepper

To serve (optional)
Greek yoghurt
Drizzle of pomegranate molasses

This is flavoured with scented spices and sweet-and-sour notes. It's a fabulous way to cook with a meat-free mince as it adds a really punchy depth to it and enhances the texture. Serve this on its own or with some warmed flatbreads, spooned into lettuce leaves or with a jacket potato or sweet potato jacket, rice or grains.

1. Heat the oil in a frying pan, add the onion, season well and cook for a couple of minutes, then add the garlic and cook for a minute more. Stir in the turmeric, cumin, cinnamon, sumac and pul biber or chilli flakes and transfer everything to the slow cooker.

2. Add the veg mince, walnuts, apricots and tomato purée and stir, then pour in the stock and stir again. Put the lid on and cook on High for 3 hours.

3. Stir through the coriander and serve with a dollop of yoghurt and a drizzle of pomegranate molasses, if wished. Serve with basmati or brown rice.

Polish pickle soup

SERVES 4–6
PREP 20 MINS
COOK 8 HOURS ON LOW

1 tbsp olive oil
1 onion, finely chopped
3 cloves garlic, finely chopped
3 sticks celery, finely chopped
4 carrots, diced
200g gherkins, cut into bite-sized pieces
500g potatoes, peeled and cut into bite-sized pieces
Large handful of dill leaves, finely chopped, reserve some for garnish
½ white or green cabbage, trimmed and finely shredded
800ml hot vegetable stock
300ml sour cream
Sea salt and freshly ground black pepper

A tangy pot of deliciousness, both warming and filling and something a little different. Really good served with some rye bread.

1. Heat the oil in a frying pan, add the onion, season well and cook for a minute, then stir in the garlic and celery and cook for a couple of minutes more, being careful not to burn the garlic.

2. Transfer the contents of the pan to the slow cooker. Add the carrot, gherkins, potato, dill, cabbage and stock. Put the lid on, set on Low and cook for 8 hours.

3. Stir in the sour cream for the last hour of cooking. Taste and season some more if needed. Garnish with the reserved dill before serving.

Vegetable goulash

SERVES 4
PREP 20 MINS
COOK 6 HOURS ON HIGH

1 tbsp olive oil
2 onions, finely sliced into rings, reserve a few for garnish
3 cloves garlic, finely chopped
1 bay leaf
1 tsp caraway seeds
2 tsp paprika
1 tsp smoked paprika
2 potatoes, peeled and cut into bite-sized pieces
2 parsnips, peeled and cut into bite-sized pieces
250g chestnut mushrooms, quartered
3 tomatoes, diced
1 tbsp tomato purée
1 tsp Dijon mustard
600ml hot mushroom or vegetable stock
Sea salt and freshly ground black pepper

To serve
Generous drizzle of sour cream
Pinch of paprika
Handful of flat-leaf parsley leaves

Sweet paprika and caraway add warming pops of flavour to this goulash. You can mix the vegetables up to your preference.

1 Heat the oil in a frying pan, add the onion, season well and cook for a minute, then stir in the garlic and bay leaf and cook for a further minute. Stir in the caraway and paprika spices and cook for a few seconds.

2 Transfer the contents of the pan to the slow cooker. Add the potato, parsnip, mushrooms, tomato, tomato purée, mustard and stock and stir well. Put the lid on, set on High and cook for 6 hours.

3 Top with reserved raw onion, a drizzle of sour cream, sprinkling of paprika and the parsley to serve.

'Faux duck' hoisin

SERVES 4
PREP 15 MINS
COOK 2 HOURS ON HIGH

6 tbsp dark soy sauce
4 cloves garlic, grated
1 tbsp dark brown sugar
1 tbsp rice vinegar
2 tbsp black rice vinegar
1 tbsp smooth peanut butter
1–2 tsp gochujang chilli paste (as per your heat preference)
2 tbsp white miso (sweet)
1 tsp ground Chinese 5-spice
2 tbsp maple syrup
1 tbsp sesame oil

200ml hot water
300g pack of frozen vegetarian shredded hoisin 'duck', defrosted

To serve
Rice paper pancakes, spring roll wrappers or Chinese-style pancakes, heated in the microwave as per the pack instructions.
1 cucumber, halved lengthways, seeds removed and sliced into fine sticks
Bunch of spring onions, trimmed and finely sliced lengthways

This is a delicious take on hoisin sauce made by grabbing things from the store cupboard. It's served here with the 'faux duck' and pancakes, but you could easily stir through some spinach and ready-to-wok style noodles at the end for a different style of supper dish.

1. Add all the sauce ingredients and hot water into the slow cooker and give it a stir. Put the lid on and cook on High for 2 hours.

2. After 1½ hours, give the sauce a stir – you may need a balloon whisk to make it smooth. Add the 'faux duck', put the lid back on and cook it for the final half hour. Loosen with a little hot water from the kettle if needed.

3. To serve, spoon a little of the mix down the middle of a warmed pancake or wrapper, top with cucumber and spring onion slices, roll and eat!

Mung bean and paneer curry

SERVES 6
PREP 20 MINS
COOK 7 HOURS ON LOW

1 tbsp olive oil
1 large onion, finely chopped
3 cloves garlic, finely chopped
5cm piece of fresh ginger, peeled and finely chopped
1 green chilli, deseeded and finely chopped
2 tsp ground turmeric
1 tbsp curry leaves, crushed
1 tbsp coriander seeds, crushed
5 green cardamom pods, crushed and seeds removed
2 tsp cumin seeds, crushed
2 tbsp garam masala
1 tbsp tomato purée
6 tomatoes, diced
400g dried mung beans, rinsed
900ml hot vegetable stock
1 cinnamon stick
225g paneer, chopped into small cubes
220g baby spinach leaves
Juice of 1 lemon
Sea salt and freshly ground black pepper

A delicious, lightly spiced curry made with a base of mung beans (moong dal), which you can order online if you can't find them in the supermarket. The beauty of using the slow cooker here is that you don't have to pre-soak the mung beans before cooking. Silky soft paneer and spinach are stirred through to serve.

1. Heat the oil in a frying pan, add the onion, season well and cook for a couple of minutes, then add the garlic, ginger and chilli and cook for a minute more. Stir through the turmeric, curry leaves, coriander seeds, cardamom seeds, cumin seeds and garam masala.

2. Transfer the contents of the pan to the slow cooker. Add the tomato purée, fresh tomatoes, mung beans and stock, give it a stir, add the cinnamon stick and put the lid on. Cook on Low for 7 hours.

3. For the last hour, add the paneer, stir, put the lid back on and continue cooking until the mung beans are tender. When ready, stir in the spinach until wilted and squeeze in the lemon juice until the flavour is just right. Serve with rice and naan or chapatti.

Squash and potato dauphinoise

SERVES 4–6
PREP 20 MINS
COOK 5 HOURS ON LOW

1 tbsp olive oil
1 large onion, finely sliced into half-moons
Generous pinch of grated nutmeg
4 cloves garlic, finely sliced
2 sage leaves, finely chopped
A few thyme sprigs, leaves only
1 small butternut squash, halved, peeled, deseeded and very finely sliced into half-moons
2 potatoes (200g), very finely sliced into half-moons
450ml double cream
100g Gruyère, grated
Sea salt and freshly ground black pepper

Tender layers of butternut squash, potato and onion are slow-cooked in a garlicky and herb cream sauce and topped off with nutty Gruyère. Enjoy on its own with a winter salad or serve as a side dish.

1. Heat the oil in a large frying pan, add the onion, season well and cook for 1 minute, then stir in the nutmeg, garlic, sage and thyme and cook for a minute more.

2. Stir in the squash and potato and turn to coat, then transfer it all to the slow cooker and pat it down so it is flat.

3. Pour over the cream, making sure everything is just immersed, then top with the Gruyère. Put the lid on and cook on Low for 5 hours.

Middle-Eastern chickpea stew

SERVES 4–6
PREP 20 MINS
COOK 8 HOURS ON LOW

2 tbsp olive oil
1 onion, finely chopped
5 cloves garlic, finely sliced
1 tsp ground turmeric
1 tsp ground cumin
1 tsp ground cinnamon
1 tsp ground coriander
Pinch of saffron, mixed with a little hot water
200g dried chickpeas, rinsed
2 leeks, trimmed, washed and sliced
½ swede, halved, peeled and cut into bite-sized pieces
3 carrots, diced
Pinch of chilli flakes
Drizzle of maple syrup
500ml passata
400ml hot vegetable stock
Juice of 1 lemon
Bunch of flat-leaf parsley, finely chopped
Pinch of za'atar
Sea salt and freshly ground black pepper

A jumble of vegetables, chickpeas and spices cook gently in the pot to produce a really tasty, healthy supper. Great served with bulgur wheat and/or some warmed flatbreads.

1. Heat the oil in a frying pan, add the onion, season well and cook for a couple of minutes, then add the garlic and cook for a minute more. Stir in the ground spices and cook them for a few seconds.

2. Transfer the contents of the pan to the slow cooker. Now add in the saffron and water, chickpeas, leek, swede, carrot, chilli flakes and maple syrup, give it a stir, then add the passata and hot stock and stir again.

3. Sit the lid on and cook for 8 hours on Low or until the chickpeas are tender. Add the lemon juice, taste and season some more, if needed. Stir in the parsley and sprinkle with the za'atar. Serve with bulgur wheat and warmed flatbreads.

Dried fruit pilaf

SERVES 6
PREP 15 MINS
COOK 4 HOURS ON HIGH

1 tbsp olive oil
1 red onion, roughly chopped
3 cloves garlic, finely chopped
1–2 green chillies, deseeded and finely chopped
1 tsp ground turmeric
1 tsp ground cinnamon
Generous grating of nutmeg
100g dried mango
100g prunes, chopped
100g sultanas or cranberries
250g quick-cook spelt, rinsed
200g rice and wild rice mix, rinsed
200g whole almonds, skin on
700ml hot vegetable stock
200g cavolo nero or kale, any chunky stalks removed, leaves shredded
2 oranges, segmented, or a handful of pomegranate seeds (optional)
Handful of flat-leaf parsley, finely chopped
Sea salt and freshly ground black pepper

This is a meal on its own, or serve it as a side with one of the stew-style dishes. It's sweet and earthy and full of colour. You can mix and match your choice of fruit and nuts.

1 Heat the oil in a frying pan, add the onion, season well and cook for a couple of minutes, then stir through the garlic and chilli and cook for a minute more. Stir through the turmeric, cinnamon and nutmeg.

2 Transfer the contents of the pan to the slow cooker. Now add the mango, prunes and sultanas, then stir through the spelt, rice, almonds and stock. Add the cavolo nero or kale a little at a time, stirring and pushing it into the mix. Put the lid on and set on High for 4 hours.

3 Check the rice is cooked – you can top up with a tiny amount of hot water from the kettle if it is too dry. Give it a stir and serve the pilaf topped with the orange segments or pomegranate seeds, if using, and parsley.

Mushroom ragu with pappardelle

SERVES 4–6
PREP 15 MINS
COOK 3½ HOURS
ON HIGH

1 tbsp olive oil
1 onion, finely chopped
4 cloves garlic, finely chopped
2 sticks celery, finely chopped
A few thyme sprigs
1kg chestnut mushrooms, finely chopped
10g porcini mushrooms (soaked in hot water for 15 mins, drained and chopped)
1 tbsp tomato purée
1 tsp Dijon mustard
1 tbsp capers, chopped
500ml passata
300ml hot vegetable stock
Pinch of chilli flakes
400g egg pappardelle
Sea salt and freshly ground black pepper

This has a really deep, rich flavour. Here the ragu is tossed with pasta, but it would be equally good spooned over a hot jacket spud or served with rice. It's a good make-ahead dish that will sit happily in the fridge for a few days while the flavours get to mature.

1. Heat the oil in a frying pan, add the onion, season well and cook for a minute, then stir in the garlic, celery and thyme and cook for a couple of minutes more.

2. Transfer the contents of the pan to the slow cooker. Add both kinds of mushrooms, the tomato purée, mustard, capers, passata, stock and chilli flakes. Stir, sit the lid on, set on High and cook for 3½ hours.

3. Add the pasta for the last 15 minutes, pushing it in and under the sauce, and cook until just tender. Alternatively, cook the pasta in a pan of boiling salted water for 6–8 minutes or as per the pack instructions and toss with the sauce.

4.
Warming & Hearty

Beetroot, orange and rosemary soup with whipped feta

SERVES 4–6
PREP 20 MINS
COOK 8 HOURS ON LOW

1 onion, chopped
2 cloves garlic, chopped
Generous pinch of chilli flakes
3 sticks celery, chopped
2 medium potatoes, peeled and chopped
A few rosemary sprigs, leaves picked
800g (1 bunch) beetroot, trimmed, peeled and chopped (whole and unpeeled for oven method)
700ml hot vegetable stock
Juice of 1 orange
Sea salt and freshly ground black pepper

For the topping
100g feta, crumbled
3 tbsp Greek yoghurt
Fresh dill leaves, for garnish
Chilli oil, to serve (optional)

This vibrant main-meal soup is a feast for the eyes. A hint of chilli really brings this to life and the addition of tangy feta makes it a little more special. Hardy beetroot is the perfect vegetable for slow cooking!

1 Add the onion, garlic, seasoning, chilli flakes, celery, potato, rosemary, beetroot, stock and orange juice to the slow cooker and give everything a stir. Cover with the lid and set on Low for 8 hours.

2 After 8 hours, all of the veg should be tender. Blitz with a stick blender to your desired consistency (I like a little texture), then ladle into soup bowls.

3 Whip together the feta and Greek yoghurt, then spoon the mixture over the soup and garnish with fresh dill and a drizzle of chilli oil, if using. Serve with sourdough or walnut bread alongside for dunking.

Tempeh stew with sherry vinegar, star anise and prunes

SERVES 4
PREP 15 MINS
COOK 6 HOURS ON HIGH

1 tbsp olive oil
1 onion, roughly chopped
3 cloves garlic, sliced
A few rosemary leaves, chopped
200g tempeh, chopped into bite-sized pieces
2 star anise
1 tbsp sherry vinegar
300g carrots, roughly chopped into chunky pieces
3 leeks, trimmed, washed and cut into chunky pieces
1 tbsp tomato purée
1 tsp English mustard
150g soft prunes, any large ones chopped
700ml hot vegetable stock
Sea salt and freshly ground black pepper

A deep, rich and sweet stew full of umami flavours and so good ladled over a jacket potato in the winter. Tempeh, which is fermented soya beans, works so well in the slow cooker as it retains its texture but absorbs all the juices from the long, slow cooking.

1. Heat the olive oil in a large frying pan, add the onion, season well and cook for a couple of minutes, then add the garlic, rosemary and tempeh and cook for a further 5 minutes until the tempeh is just beginning to colour. Add the star anise and sherry vinegar and turn the heat up. Let the vinegar bubble for a minute, then transfer it all to the slow cooker.

2. Add the carrot, leek, tomato purée, mustard, prunes and hot stock, put the lid on and cook on High for 6 hours. Taste and season again, if needed, then serve with a hot buttered jacket potato or rice.

Portobello mushroom stew with dumplings

SERVES 4
PREP 20 MINS
COOK 5 HOURS ON HIGH

1 tbsp olive oil
1 onion, finely chopped
2 sticks celery, finely chopped
2 carrots, diced
3 cloves garlic, chopped
4 medium potatoes, peeled and cut into bite-sized pieces
1 tbsp tomato purée
1 tbsp smooth peanut butter
2 tbsp tamari or dark soy sauce
2 tsp paprika
Handful of thyme sprigs

700ml hot mushroom or vegetable stock
4 Portobello mushrooms, thickly sliced
Sea salt and freshly ground black pepper
Handful of parsley leaves, for garnish (optional)

For the dumplings (makes 12)
175g self-raising flour
50g butter
20g vegetarian Parmesan, grated
2–3 tbsp cold water

A rich stew for a cold day. The magic mix of onion, carrots and celery is pan-fried first to add more depth of flavour to the stew. The meaty mushrooms are added to the pot later so they retain their shape.

1 Heat the olive oil in a frying pan and add the onion, celery and carrot and season well. Cook for about 5 minutes, until starting to soften, then stir through the garlic and cook for 1 minute more.

2 Transfer the contents of the pan to the slow cooker along with the potatoes, tomato purée, peanut butter, tamari or soy sauce, paprika, thyme and stock. Stir to combine, then put the lid on and set for 5 hours on High.

3 With just over an hour to go, make the dumplings. Put the flour in a large bowl and season well, then rub the butter into the flour using your fingertips until it resembles breadcrumbs. Stir through the Parmesan. Slowly add the cold water a little at a time and begin to gently pull the mixture together to incorporate the water – when it's ready it should all come away from the side of the bowl. Try not to overhandle so that it remains light. Cut it into 12 equal pieces and roll into balls.

4 After 4 hours of cooking time, add the mushrooms and the dumplings to the stew, gently pushing them into the liquid. If it seems too thick, add a little hot water from the kettle. Put the lid on and leave to cook for 1 more hour, until the mushrooms are tender and the dumplings are light and fluffy. Garnish with parsley leaves if you wish and serve piping hot straight to the table with some crusty bread on the side to mop up the juices.

WARMING & HEARTY

Leek and pink peppercorn risotto with Shropshire Blue

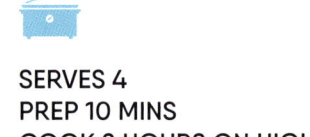

SERVES 4
PREP 10 MINS
COOK 2 HOURS ON HIGH

1 tbsp olive oil
50g butter
1 onion, finely chopped
3 cloves garlic, finely chopped
3 chunky leeks, trimmed, washed and sliced
½ wine glass of white wine or rosé
2 tbsp pink peppercorns, lightly crushed (reserve a few for garnish)
400g Arborio risotto rice
700ml hot vegetable stock
150g Shropshire Blue or Stilton, crumbled
Sea salt and freshly ground black pepper

Stilton feels right for winter, and it's usually knocking around the fridge at this time of year. In fact, a risotto is a really good choice of meal when ingredients are low. Providing you've got risotto rice in the store cupboard, you can get really inventive and use pretty much any vegetable and cheese in the mix.

1. Heat the oil and butter in a frying pan, add the onion and season well, then cook for a couple of minutes. Add the garlic and leeks and cook for a further couple of minutes, then add the wine. Let it bubble, then transfer it all to the slow cooker.

2. Stir in the peppercorns and rice so it all gets well coated, then add the stock and stir again. Put the lid on and set on High for 2 hours.

3. Check the rice is cooked, then stir through the Shropshire Blue or Stilton, leaving a little to sprinkle on top. Scatter over the remaining pink peppercorns and blue cheese to serve.

Mac and cheese with butternut squash

SERVES 4–6
PREP 15 MINS
COOK 4 HOURS ON HIGH,
THEN 1½ HOURS ON LOW

Splash of olive oil
1 butternut squash, halved, deseeded, peeled and cubed
500g macaroni (soaked in boiling water for 5 mins and drained)
600ml full-fat milk
1 tbsp butter
1 tbsp plain flour (for oven method)
165g full-fat cream cheese
100g strong Cheddar cheese, grated
1 tsp Dijon mustard
1 large red onion, diced (soaked in water for 5 mins and drained)
Sea salt and freshly ground black pepper

For the topping (optional)
Splash of olive oil
Handful of sage leaves
Pinch of paprika

This is super creamy with the addition of squash, although if you want to speed things up, you don't have to add it. The red onion stirred through before serving adds a welcome hint of texture. Remember to switch the setting to Low when adding the pasta and sauce as dairy has a tendency to split if the temperature is too high.

1. Drizzle the olive oil around the slow cooker, then add the butternut squash, season well, put the lid on and set on High for 4 hours. When it's ready, turn the setting to Low.

2. Add the pasta, milk, butter, cream cheese, grated cheese and mustard and give it a stir. Season, put the lid on and cook on Low for 1½ hours until the pasta is cooked. Stir through the red onion.

3. If using the sage leaves, heat the oil in a frying pan, add the sage leaves and cook for a few minutes until crisp.

4. Top the macaroni cheese with crispy sage leaves, if using, and a pinch of paprika. Serve with a winter leaf salad or steamed spinach to cut through the richness.

Leek and potato chunky soup with Stilton toasties

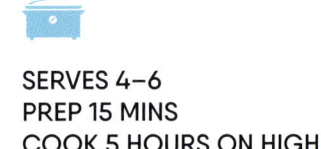

SERVES 4–6
PREP 15 MINS
COOK 5 HOURS ON HIGH

1 tbsp olive oil
1 onion, chopped
3 cloves garlic, finely chopped
2 sage leaves, finely chopped
Splash of dry cider (optional)
4 large leeks, trimmed, washed and finely sliced
3 potatoes, peeled and cut into bite-sized pieces
700ml hot vegetable stock
2 tsp Dijon mustard
Sea salt and freshly ground black pepper

To serve
½ sourdough loaf, sliced
100g Stilton, roughly grated

This is proper cold-weather food. Stilton toasties make use of any leftover festive Stilton lurking in the fridge. And to liven this dish up, stir a spoonful of horseradish sauce or a grating of fresh horseradish into the soup. For a creamy version, stir in some crème fraîche or single cream before serving and warm through.

1 Heat the oil in a frying pan, add the onion, season well and cook for a couple of minutes, then add the garlic and cook for a minute more. Stir in the sage leaves and add the cider, if using, bringing to a bubble for a minute or two.

2 Transfer the contents of the pan to the slow cooker. Add the leek, potato, stock and mustard, stir and put the lid on and set on High for 5 hours. Taste and season some more if needed.

3 To make the toasties, toast one side of the slices of bread under a hot grill, flip and cover with Stilton and toast until bubbling. Sit them on top of the soup to serve.

Parsnip and carrot tagine with ginger and rhubarb topping

SERVES 4
PREP 20 MINS
COOK 4 HOURS ON HIGH

4 sticks rhubarb, chopped
10cm piece of fresh ginger, peeled and grated
Pinch of brown sugar (optional)
2 tbsp olive oil
3 cloves garlic, finely chopped
2 tsp ground turmeric
1 tsp ground cumin
2 tsp paprika
2 tsp harissa
Bunch of flat-leaf parsley, finely chopped

100ml water
1 red onion, finely chopped
400g tin of chopped tomatoes
1 sweet potato, peeled and chopped
3 parsnips, peeled and cut into large batons
½ cauliflower, broken into florets
3 carrots, cut into large batons
Handful of pitted green olives
Sea salt and freshly ground black pepper

This dish has a delicious sweet, spicy and tangy flavour through it and goes so well served with bulgur wheat or some brown rice. The vegetables are layered and then stew lightly in the slow cooker.

1 First, prepare the rhubarb. Put the chopped rhubarb pieces and half the ginger in a small pan, add about 1 tablespoon of water and sweeten with a pinch of brown sugar, if you wish. Simmer for a few minutes until tender, then put to one side.

2 In a bowl, mix together 1 tablespoon of the olive oil, the garlic, turmeric, remaining ginger, cumin, paprika, harissa and half the finely chopped parsley. Stir in the 100ml of water.

3 Heat the remaining oil in a frying pan, add the onion, season well and cook for a couple of minutes, then add the contents of the pan to the slow cooker along with the tinned tomatoes. Give it a stir, then layer the vegetables into the pot with a spoonful of the spice mixture as you go. Put the lid on and set on High for 4 hours.

4 Stir through the olives and top with the remaining parsley and the rhubarb to serve.

Celeriac, tamarind and peanut stew with apple salsa

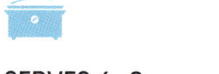

SERVES 6–8
PREP 15 MINS
COOK 4 HOURS ON HIGH

1 tbsp olive oil
1 onion, finely chopped
2 cloves garlic, finely chopped
2 sticks celery, chopped
Handful of thyme sprigs, leaves only, reserve some for garnish
1 celeriac, peeled and chopped
1 tbsp tamarind pulp mixed with a little hot water or 1 tbsp tamarind paste
1 tbsp peanut butter
1 tsp Dijon mustard

400g tin of butter beans, drained
600ml hot vegetable stock
Large handful of spinach leaves
Sea salt and freshly ground black pepper

For the topping
2 sweet red-skinned apples, diced
Handful of flat-leaf parsley, finely chopped
Handful of salted peanuts, roughly chopped

Celeriac calls for some gutsy flavours in this stew. It's topped with chopped apple and a scattering of peanuts, which give it a fabulous 'crunch' and freshness. Serve with brown rice or bulgur wheat or spoon over a hot jacket potato.

1. Heat the oil in a frying pan, add the onion, season well and cook for a minute, then stir in the garlic, celery and thyme leaves and cook for a further minute.

2. Transfer the contents of the pan to the slow cooker. Add the celeriac, tamarind, peanut butter, mustard and butter beans and stir, then pour in the stock and stir again. Put the lid on, set on High and cook for 4 hours or until the celeriac is tender. Top up with a little hot water if it needs it. Stir through the spinach until it wilts.

3. Toss the apple with the parsley and a pinch of sea salt and scatter over the stew. Top with peanuts to serve.

Jerusalem artichoke and potato stew with clementine and parsley gremolata topping

SERVES 4
PREP 20 MINS
COOK 8 HOURS ON LOW

1 tbsp olive oil
1 red onion, finely chopped
1 tsp dried oregano
A few rosemary sprigs, leaves picked and chopped
4 cloves garlic, finely sliced
Peel and juice of 1 clementine or similar
600g Jerusalem artichokes, washed and sliced, no need to peel! (use parsnips if you can't get the artichokes)
4 potatoes (400g), peeled and cut into bite-sized pieces
15g porcini mushrooms (soaked in hot water for 30 mins, drained and chopped, strain and reserve the juice and mix with the stock)
500ml hot mushroom or vegetable stock
Sea salt and freshly ground black pepper

For the topping (optional)
Handful of flat-leaf parsley, finely chopped
Zest of 1 clementine
2 cloves garlic, grated

Jerusalem artichokes' woody flavour works really well with earthy potatoes. They are in season during the winter months, so grab them while you can. The clementine topping is optional, but it's a nice contrast to this hearty stew.

1. Heat the olive oil in a frying pan, add the onion, season well and cook for a minute, then add the oregano, rosemary and garlic and cook for a minute more.

2. Transfer the contents of the pan to the slow cooker. Add the peel and juice of the clementine, the Jerusalem artichokes, potato, porcini mushrooms and reserved juice and stock. Give it a stir, put the lid on and set on Low for 8 hours or until the potatoes are tender.

3. To serve, mix the parsley, clementine zest, garlic and a sprinkle of sea salt together and top the stew, or just top with chopped parsley if you prefer.

Irish stew

SERVES 4–6
PREP 20 MINS
COOK 8 HOURS ON LOW

1 tbsp olive oil
1 onion, roughly chopped
3 cloves garlic, finely chopped
2 rosemary sprigs, leaves picked and finely chopped
2 sticks celery, finely chopped
300ml Guinness
450g potatoes, peeled and cut into bite-sized pieces
4 carrots, roughly chopped
2 turnips, peeled and cut into bite-sized pieces
2 leeks, trimmed, washed and finely sliced
300g button mushrooms
1 tbsp tomato purée
2 tsp brown sugar (optional)
100g dried red lentils, rinsed
300ml hot vegetable stock
Sea salt and freshly ground black pepper

A hugely warming and nourishing pot, this is a good stew to use up any leftover vegetables lurking about and you can mix and match your favourites. It's important to give the Guinness a bubble first as it can be too bitter if added straight to the slow cooker.

1. Heat the oil in a frying pan, add the onion, season well and cook for a minute, then stir in the garlic, rosemary and celery and cook for a minute more. Raise the heat, pour in the Guinness and let it bubble for a few minutes.

2. Transfer the contents of the pan to the slow cooker. Add the potato, carrot, turnip, leek, mushrooms, tomato purée, brown sugar, if using, and lentils and stir, then add the stock and stir again.

3. Put the lid on, set on Low and cook for 8 hours. Serve with some crusty bread on the side.

Portuguese-style potato and three greens soup

SERVES 4–6
PREP 20 MINS
COOK 5 HOURS ON HIGH

2 tbsp olive oil (extra needed for oven method)
1 onion, finely chopped
4 cloves garlic, finely sliced
6 medium waxy potatoes, peeled and roughly chopped
700ml hot vegetable stock
Bunch of kale, any chunky stalks removed, leaves finely shredded
1 dark green cabbage, trimmed and leaves finely shredded
Bunch of spring greens, finely shredded
Pinch of chilli flakes, plus extra for serving
Sea salt and freshly ground black pepper

Based on the Portuguese caldo verde, here a few humble winter ingredients really do taste great. The soup is guaranteed to restore and it certainly makes you feel righteous! It relies on cooking the potatoes until they soften in the oil and then melt into the stock, so use waxy ones, don't overcook the finely shredded cabbage and add a good amount of seasoning.

1. Heat half the olive oil in a large heavy-based deep pan, add the onion, season well and cook for a couple of minutes, then stir in the garlic and cook for a further minute.

2. Transfer the contents of the pan to the slow cooker. Add the potatoes and the remaining oil, season, put the lid on and set on High for 5 hours.

3. After 2 hours, add the stock, all the greens and the chilli flakes, put the lid on and continue cooking for the last 3 hours. Top up with a little hot water if it seems dry, taste and season some more as needed. Serve topped with a pinch of chilli flakes and some crusty bread on the side.

Slow-cooked sprouts, red onion and garlic with a lemon and tahini dressing

SERVES 4
PREP 20 MINS
COOK 3 HOURS ON HIGH

Drizzle of olive oil
1 large red onion, roughly chopped
4 cloves garlic, finely sliced
A few thyme sprigs, leaves only
800g Brussels sprouts, trimmed and halved
2 tsp white miso (sweet)
Generous drizzle of maple syrup
Handful of flaked almonds
Sea salt and freshly ground black pepper

For the topping
2 tbsp tahini
Juice of 1 lemon

This is a really punchy mix of flavours – sweet miso and maple syrup with bitter sprouts and a nutty topping. Serve as a side or as a main with a wild rice mix or bulgur wheat.

1. Heat the oil in a frying pan, add the onion, season well and cook for a minute, then stir in the garlic and thyme and cook for a minute more.

2. Transfer the contents of the pan to the slow cooker. Stir in the sprouts, miso and maple syrup. Put the lid on, set on High and cook for 3 hours. Add the flaked almonds for the last 15 minutes of cooking.

3. Mix the tahini and lemon juice together, then whisk in warm water until it makes a 'dressing' consistency. Season to taste and drizzle over the sprouts to serve.

Red cabbage with ginger beer topped with dates and Stilton

SERVES 6
PREP 15 MINS
COOK 5 HOURS ON HIGH

1 tbsp olive oil
1 red onion, finely chopped
2 cloves garlic, finely chopped
5cm piece of fresh ginger, peeled and grated
2 apples, peeled and cut into bite-sized pieces
1 red cabbage, trimmed and shredded
250ml non-alcoholic ginger beer
50ml cider vinegar
Handful of sultanas
1 tbsp brown sugar
2 star anise
1 cinnamon stick
Handful of dates, chopped (optional)
100g Stilton, crumbled (optional)
Sea salt and freshly ground black pepper

This can be enjoyed on its own as it is or, for a more substantial supper dish, serve it with some brown or wild rice or rye bread.

1. Heat the oil in a frying pan, add the onion, season well and cook for a minute, then stir in the garlic and ginger and cook for a minute more.

2. Transfer the contents of the pan to the slow cooker. Add the apple, cabbage, ginger beer, vinegar, sultanas, brown sugar, star anise and cinnamon stick.

3. Put the lid on, set on High and cook for 5 hours. Taste and season some more if needed. Serve topped with dates and Stilton, if using.

Italian ribollita

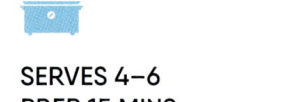

SERVES 4–6
PREP 15 MINS
COOK 8 HOURS ON LOW

1 tbsp olive oil
1 onion, chopped
3 cloves garlic, chopped
Pinch of chilli flakes
3 sticks celery, diced
3 carrots, diced
Piece of vegetarian Parmesan rind or use 2 tsp yeast flakes, plus extra grated Parmesan for serving
400g tin of cannellini beans, drained
400g tin of borlotti beans, drained
250g cavolo nero, any chunky stalks removed
700ml hot vegetable stock mixed with 1 tbsp tomato purée
Sea salt and freshly ground black pepper
Drizzle of balsamic vinegar and extra virgin olive oil, for serving (optional)

This Italian-style one-pot is the ultimate in make-ahead for maximum flavour. It's the dish that keeps on giving: cheap, nutritious, filling and super tasty!

1. Heat the oil in a frying pan, add the onion, season and cook for a minute, then stir in the garlic, chilli flakes and celery and cook for a couple of minutes more.

2. Transfer the contents of the pan to the slow cooker. Add the carrot, Parmesan rind or yeast flakes, both kinds of beans and the cavolo nero. Pour over the stock mixture and squash everything down so it is all immersed. Put the lid on, set on Low and cook for 8 hours. Top up with a little hot water from the kettle if needed.

3. To serve, top with the Parmesan and the balsamic vinegar and oil, if using.

Yellow split pea soup with yoghurt and toasted almonds

SERVES 4–6
PREP 10 MINS
COOK 9 HOURS ON LOW

1 tbsp olive oil
1 onion, finely chopped
3 cloves garlic, finely chopped
5cm piece of fresh ginger, peeled and grated
1 tbsp garam masala
2 tsp ground turmeric
400g yellow split peas, rinsed
500ml passata
600ml hot vegetable stock
Sea salt and freshly ground black pepper

For the topping
Greek yoghurt
Handful of toasted almonds

Serve this as a soup or with rice and some naan bread for a substantial supper dish. The toppings are optional, and you could also garnish with lots of fried sweet onions or stir through some spinach if you wish.

1. Heat the oil in a frying pan, add the onion, season well and cook for a minute, then add the garlic and ginger and cook for a further minute. Stir in the spices and let them cook for a few seconds.

2. Transfer the contents of the pan to the slow cooker. Add the split peas and stir, then stir in the passata and the stock.

3. Sit the lid on, set on Low and cook for 9 hours or until the split peas are tender. Top up with a little hot water from the kettle if needed. Serve topped with the yoghurt and toasted almonds.

Pottage pie

SERVES 4
PREP 15 MINS
COOK 5 HOURS ON HIGH

1 tbsp olive oil
1 onion, finely chopped
3 cloves garlic, finely chopped
2 sticks celery, diced
1 tsp dried oregano
1 tsp ground cinnamon
1 tsp ground cumin
250g dried green or brown lentils, rinsed
2 carrots, diced
1 tbsp tomato purée
2 tsp yeast extract
700ml hot vegetable stock
Sea salt and freshly ground black pepper

For the topping
2–3 sweet potatoes, peeled and very finely sliced (600g)
50g butter, diced
100g mature Cheddar cheese, grated

The rich lentil base is simmered slowly first, then topped with sweet potato and grated cheese – real comfort food!

1. Heat the oil in a frying pan, add the onion, season well and cook for a minute, then add the garlic and celery and cook for a minute more. Stir in the oregano, cinnamon and cumin and cook for a few seconds. Transfer it all to the slow cooker.

2. Add the lentils, carrot, tomato purée and yeast extract and stir well, then pour over the stock and stir again. Put the lid on, set to High and cook for 5 hours.

3. After 3 hours of cooking, the lentils should be tender. Top up with a little hot water if at all dry, then top the lentils with the potato and dot with butter. Put the lid back on and cook for a further 2 hours, adding the grated cheese for the final hour.

Black-eyed beans spicy pot with polenta dumplings

SERVES 4–6
PREP 20 MINS
COOK 9 HOURS ON LOW

1 tbsp olive oil
1 red onion, finely chopped
Bunch of spring onions, trimmed and finely chopped
4 cloves garlic, finely chopped
1 green chilli, deseeded and finely chopped
1 tsp each whole allspice and coriander seeds, pounded in a pestle and mortar
Pinch of grated nutmeg
250g dried black-eyed beans, rinsed
400g tin of chopped tomatoes
600ml hot vegetable stock
Sea salt and freshly ground black pepper
Handful of coriander leaves, chopped, for garnish (optional)

For the polenta dumplings
150g self-raising flour
120g polenta
50g mature Cheddar cheese, grated
1 egg
120ml milk

Dumplings really transport this beany dish, adding another level of texture. You could up the spice and add chilli to the dumpling mix.

1. Heat the oil in a frying pan, add the onion and spring onion, season well and cook for a minute, then stir in the garlic and chilli and cook for a minute more. Stir in the spices and cook for a few seconds, then transfer it all to the slow cooker.

2. Add the beans, tomatoes and stock and stir, put the lid on and set on Low for 9 hours.

3. To make the dumplings, put the flour and polenta in a bowl, season, add the cheese and egg and trickle in the milk. Stir gently and pull it all together until combined.

4. After 8 hours, check the beans are tender; if not, cook a little longer. Add the dumplings for the last 1 hour of cooking, spooning in about 12 dollops of the mixture, then sit the lid back on. Garnish with coriander, if using.

Kashmiri veggie mince curry with cucumber pickle

SERVES 4–6
PREP 15 MINS
COOK 4 HOURS ON HIGH

1 tbsp olive oil
1 onion, finely chopped
4 cloves garlic, finely chopped
1 red chilli, deseeded and finely chopped
5cm piece of fresh ginger, peeled and finely chopped
1 tsp tandoori spice
1 tsp ground turmeric
1 tsp ground cumin
1 cinnamon stick
3 potatoes (400g), diced
3 tomatoes, diced
454g pack (or similar weight) plant-based mince
1 tbsp tomato purée
700ml hot vegetable stock
Juice of 1 lemon
Bunch of coriander, leaves chopped, for garnish
Sea salt and freshly ground black pepper
Cucumber pickle, to serve (see page 34)

Hot and spicy plant-based mince cooks slowly here with potatoes and stock. The pickle is a great addition to cut through the richness, but yoghurt or chutney would also be delicious along with a naan bread.

1. Heat the oil in a frying pan, add the onion, season well and cook for a minute, then stir in the garlic, chilli and ginger and cook for a minute more. Stir through the ground spices and cook for a few minutes.

2. Transfer the contents of the pan to the slow cooker. Now add the cinnamon stick, potato, tomato, plant-based mince, tomato purée and stock and stir well. Put the lid on and set on High for 4 hours.

3. Taste and season some more if needed. To serve, squeeze the lemon juice in and stir through the coriander. Serve alongside the cucumber pickle.

Mulligatawny pot

SERVES 4–6
PREP 15 MINS
COOK 5 HOURS ON HIGH

1 tbsp olive oil
1 onion, finely chopped
4 cloves garlic, finely chopped
5cm piece of fresh ginger, peeled and grated
1 green chilli, deseeded and finely chopped
1 tsp mustard seeds
2 tsp garam masala
1 tsp medium curry powder
1 tsp ground turmeric
2 potatoes, peeled and diced
2 parsnips, peeled and diced
2 carrots, peeled and diced
1 apple, peeled and diced
100g dried red lentils, rinsed
500ml hot vegetable stock mixed with 1 tbsp tomato purée
1 tsp mango chutney (optional)
Juice of 1 lime (optional)
Sea salt and freshly ground black pepper
A few coriander leaves, for garnish (optional)

A wonderful, heady mix of vegetables with Indian spices. Slurp as a soup and serve with a roti or you could eat with rice.

1. Heat the oil in a frying pan, add the onion, season well and cook for a minute, then add the garlic, ginger, chilli and mustard seeds and cook for a minute more. Stir in the garam masala, curry powder and turmeric and cook for a few seconds. Transfer everything to the slow cooker.

2. Add the potato, parsnip, carrot, apple and lentils, stir well and pour over the stock mixture. Put the lid on, set on High and cook for 5 hours or until all the vegetables are tender. Top up with more hot water if needed.

3. Stir through the mango chutney and lime juice, if using. Taste and season some more if needed, then garnish with coriander, if using.

Whole 'roast' cauliflower and root vegetables

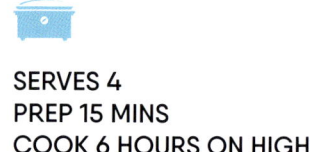

SERVES 4
PREP 15 MINS
COOK 6 HOURS ON HIGH

2 tbsp olive oil
1 red onion, roughly chopped
4 cloves garlic, finely sliced
3–4 medium potatoes, peeled and cut into bite-sized pieces
2–3 carrots, cut into bite-sized pieces
3 parsnips, peeled and cut into bite-sized pieces
1 cauliflower, leaves removed, left whole (throw a few leaves into the pot if you wish)
50g butter
A few thyme sprigs, leaves only
Drizzle of maple syrup
Sea salt and freshly ground black pepper

This is perfect to serve as part of a veggie Sunday roast, alongside some meat-free sausages, vegetarian gravy and bread or cranberry sauce.

1. Heat half the oil in a frying pan, add the onion, season well and cook for a minute, then add the garlic and cook for a minute more.

2. Transfer the contents of the pan to the slow cooker. Drizzle the remaining oil into the slow cooker, add the potato, carrot and parsnip, then sit the cauliflower among the root veg and onions, nestling it down. Dot the cauliflower with butter, thyme and maple syrup

3. Sit the lid on and set on High for 6 hours or until everything is tender. Transfer to a serving plate and serve piping hot.

5.
In the Oven & on the Hob

Please refer to the slow-cooker recipes for the list of ingredients for each method. In some cases, more stock has been used as oven/hob cooking usually requires more liquid than slow cooking.

Light & Bright

New potato and asparagus pot with goat's cheese *(page 21)*

SERVES 4
PREP 15 MINS, PLUS 2 HOURS PICKLING
COOK 50 MINS

1. Heat the oil in a large, heavy-based pan, add the onion and season well, then cook for 2 minutes. Stir in the garlic and lemon zest and cook for a few seconds more.

2. Stir in the green chilli and capers and cook for a further couple of minutes, then throw in the cannellini beans, potatoes and dill and stir well to coat.

3. Add the vegetable stock and bring to the boil, then reduce it to a simmer and cook for 30–40 minutes or until the potatoes are cooked, topping up with a little more hot water if needed. Add the green beans for the last 20 minutes of cooking, then the asparagus for the last 15 minutes, and finally stir in the peas, artichokes and most of the fresh mint at the end. Add a squeeze of lemon juice. Serve as in the slow-cooker recipe.

Saffron rice with asparagus and dill raita *(page 22)*

SERVES 4–6
PREP 5 MINS
COOK 50 MINS

1. Put the rice and butter in a large pan and cover with water so it sits about 10cm above. Stir in the saffron water mix and season well. Sit the lid ajar and cook for about 20–30 minutes or until all the water has been absorbed. Top up with a little more if it needs it.

2. Remove the pan from the heat, sit the lid on top and leave it to steam for about 15 minutes, then fluff it up with a fork.

3. While that is cooking, steam the asparagus for about 10 minutes or until tender by sitting it in a steamer or colander, sat over a pan of just simmering water with the lid on. Serve as in the slow-cooker recipe with the dill raita on the side.

Thai green curry *(page 25)*

SERVES 4–6
PREP 15 MINS
COOK 1 HOUR

1. Heat the oil in a large, heavy-based pan, add the shallots and season well. Cook for a minute, then stir in the garlic, chilli, ginger and lemongrass. Cook over a low heat for a further 5–10 minutes and stir well, then add the rest of the paste ingredients.

2. Pour in the hot vegetable stock and bring to the boil, then reduce the curry to a simmer and cook for about 15 minutes. Pour in the coconut milk and simmer gently, stirring it occasionally for about 20 minutes, then taste and adjust the seasoning as needed.

3. Throw in the mushrooms and sugar snap peas and cook for a further 5–10 minutes, then stir through the watercress and top with chilli flakes, if using. Garnish as in the slow-cooker recipe.

Singapore noodles with egg scramble *(page 26)*

SERVES 4
PREP 15 MINS
COOK 30 MINS

1. Heat the sesame oil in a large, deep frying pan or wok, add the onion, season well and cook for a couple of minutes, then add the garlic and celery and cook for a couple of minutes more.

2. Add the ginger and chilli and cook for a few more minutes then, over a high heat, add the carrot and cabbage and stir-fry for a few minutes. Add the peppers and cook for a few minutes more. Mix the curry powder with 100ml hot water or vegetable stock and pour in, then let it boil for 5 or so minutes for it to reduce.

3. Push the vegetables to one side and add the Shaoxing wine, sugar and soy and let this bubble until it thickens slightly, then toss it with the vegetables.

4. Soak the noodles in boiling water for 2 minutes or as per the pack instructions, drain well, then stir through the vegetable mix.

5. To serve, heat the butter in a frying pan, add the egg and let it spread and cook for a few seconds. Push it around the edges with a fork, being careful to not over scramble it. When ready, lift it out, roughly chop and add to the top of the noodles dish. Garnish with chives, if using.

Sweet potato, spring cabbage and fennel pot with harissa and lemon *(page 29)*

SERVES 4
PREP 20 MINS
COOK 1 HOUR 20 MINS

1. Heat the oil in a large, heavy-based, shallow pan. Add the onion, season well and cook for a couple of minutes, then stir in the garlic and bay leaf and cook for a further minute.

2. Add the fennel, cabbage and sweet potato and cook for 6–8 minutes, stirring occasionally so it doesn't catch. Stir in the za'atar, lemon zest, tomato purée and harissa paste so it all gets well coated. Add the tomatoes and stir.

3. Pour in 700ml hot vegetable stock, bring to the boil, then reduce to a simmer and cook, with the lid ajar, for about 45 minutes–1 hour or until the stock has reduced and the mixture has thickened. Taste and season some more if needed. Serve as in the slow-cooker recipe.

Spring green minestrone with orzo pasta *(page 30)*

SERVES 4–6
PREP 15 MINS
COOK 1 HOUR

1. Heat the olive oil in a large, heavy-based pan, add the spring onion, season well and cook for a couple of minutes, then add the garlic and cook for a minute more.

2. Add the cannellini beans and cabbage/greens, Parmesan rind or yeast flakes and chilli flakes and stir, then pour in 900ml hot vegetable stock. Bring to the boil and simmer for about 20 minutes, then add the broad beans and peas and simmer for a further 10–15 minutes.

3. Add the pasta and asparagus and simmer for a further 10 minutes or until the pasta is cooked. Top up with more hot stock, if needed. Stir through the pesto and serve topped with Parmesan, if using.

Pearl barley risotto with courgette and tomato

(page 33)

SERVES 4
PREP 10 MINS
COOK 1 HOUR 20 MINS

1. Heat the oil in a large, deep frying pan, add the onion, season well, and cook for a couple of minutes, then stir through the garlic and cook for a further minute.

2. Add the courgette and cook, stirring occasionally, for 8–10 minutes until tender and golden, then remove and put to one side. Add the chilli, cumin and sumac to the pan, stir and cook for a few seconds, then add the capers, sun-dried tomatoes, pearl barley, passata and vegetable stock.

3. Bring the mixture to the boil, then reduce it to a simmer and cook, with the lid ajar, for about 1 hour until the barley is tender and the flavours have melded together, topping up with hot water, if needed. Add the courgette for the last 10 minutes of cooking. Taste and season if needed. Serve as in the slow-cooker recipe.

Malaysian-style curry with sambal, aubergine and okra *(page 34)*

SERVES 4
PREP 20 MINS
COOK 1 HOUR 45 MINS

1. Heat half the olive oil in a large, deep pan, add the shallots, season well and cook for a couple of minutes, then add the garlic, chilli, lemongrass and ginger and cook for a couple more minutes.

2. Stir in the spices, curry leaves and lime zest, cook for a minute, then stir in the sambal paste, if using, mango pulp, chopped tomatoes, 700ml vegetable stock and the aubergine, coriander stalks and half the chopped leaves. Bring to the boil, then reduce to a low simmer and cook with the lid ajar for about 1–1½ hours, topping up with hot water if needed. Cook until the sauce has reduced and thickened and all the flavours have melded together. Taste and season some more if needed. Stir through the remaining chopped coriander leaves.

3. Heat the remaining olive oil in a frying pan and add the okra. Cook for 5–6 minutes or until pale golden, then tip them into the curry. Serve as in the slow-cooker recipe.

Asparagus ends soup with soft-boiled egg and cress topping

(page 37)

SERVES 4
PREP 5 MINS
COOK 30 MINS

1. Heat the olive oil in a large, heavy-based pan, add the onion, season and cook for a few minutes until soft, then stir in the garlic, asparagus ends, potato, spring onion and leek, stir and cook for 5–10 minutes until everything begins to soften.

2. Pour in 900ml hot vegetable stock, bring to the boil, then reduce it to a simmer and cook for about 15 minutes or until the potatoes are tender when poked with a sharp knife. Stir in some cream now, if using.

3. Use a stick blender to blitz the soup or pour it into a blender, then pass it through a sieve until smooth. Serve as in the slow-cooker recipe.

Brown rice and soya bean pilaf in a sweet Asian sauce *(page 38)*

SERVES 6
PREP 15 MINS
COOK 1 HOUR

1. In a large, heavy-based pan, heat the oil, add the onion and season, then cook for a couple of minutes. Stir in the garlic, lemongrass and ginger and cook for a few minutes until tender.

2. Stir in the rice and turn to coat, then pour over 900ml hot mushroom or vegetable stock and stir in soy sauce, maple syrup, sweet chilli sauce and lime. Put the lid on ajar and cook for about 30–40 minutes until the rice is tender. Top up with a little more hot water if needed.

3. Meanwhile, add the soya beans to a pan of boiling salted water and cook for about 5 minutes until tender. Drain well, then stir them into the rice. Taste and season if needed. Serve as in the slow-cooker recipe.

Mediterranean layered savoury bread-and-butter bake with feta

(page 41)

SERVES 4
PREP 20 MINS
COOK 40 MINS

1. Preheat the oven to 190°C/170°C fan/gas 5. Heat the olive oil in a frying pan, add the onion and season well. Cook for a couple of minutes, then stir in the garlic and cook for a minute more. Stir through the basil and set aside.

2. In a deep ovenproof dish, layer the bread with the onion mixture, feta and cherry tomatoes.

3. In a jug, mix the milk, eggs and oregano together and pour it over the bread layers, pushing the bread down so it is all immersed under the egg mixture. Cover with foil and bake in the oven for 30 minutes, then remove the foil and cook it for a further 5–10 minutes until golden and risen. Remove from the oven, drizzle with olive oil and garnish with basil leaves and slice to serve.

Hunter's rice with wild garlic *(page 42)*

SERVES 4
PREP 5 MINS
COOK RICE 50 MINS/GARLIC 1 HOUR

1. To roast the garlic, preheat the oven to 200°C/180°C fan/gas 6. Sit the prepared garlic on a baking sheet, drizzle over a little olive oil and roast in the oven for about 1 hour or until the garlic is soft. Remove and put to one side.

Continues overleaf >

2. While that is cooking, prepare the rice. Heat the oil in a large, deep pan, add the onion, season well and cook for a few minutes, then stir in the celery and cook for a few minutes until it begins to soften.

3. Tip in the rice and butter, pour over the hot stock, stir and leave it to simmer for about 30–40 minutes, topping up with hot water if it seems dry. Taste and season some more if needed, then stir through the wild garlic leaves or wilted spinach and the peas. Serve as in the slow-cooker recipe with the roasted garlic bulbs.

Spring carrot and chives soup *(page 45)*

SERVES 4–6
PREP 10 MINS
COOK 1 HOUR

1. Heat the olive oil in a large, deep pan, add the onion, season well and cook for a couple of minutes, then add the garlic and cook for a minute more.

2. Throw in the potatoes, carrots and chives, stir and cook for a few minutes, then pour over 1 litre hot vegetable stock. Sit the lid ajar and simmer for about 40–50 minutes or until the carrots are tender. Blitz with a stick blender, topping up with a little hot water if needed. Serve as in the slow-cooker recipe.

Braised leeks, courgettes, spring carrots and tarragon with a mustard dressing

(page 46)

SERVES 4
PREP 15 MINS
COOK 40 MINS

1. Preheat the oven to 190°C/170°C fan/gas 5. Put the leek, courgette and carrot in a large roasting tin.

2. Drizzle over the oil, dot with the butter and pour over 200ml hot vegetable stock. Throw in the tarragon and lemon strips and season well. Cover tightly with foil and cook for about 40 minutes or until the vegetables are tender.

3. Remove from the oven, drizzle over the dressing and garnish with fresh thyme or tarragon or both.

Spring veg katsu curry

(page 49)

SERVES 4
PREP 20 MINS
COOK SAUCE 40 MINS/VEGETABLES 40 MINS

1. For the sauce, heat the olive oil in a deep frying pan, add the onion, season well and cook for a few minutes until beginning to soften. Stir in the garlic, ginger, chilli, carrots and apple, stir to combine and cook for about 5–6 minutes, stirring occasionally, then add the spices and turn to coat.

2. Add the soy sauce, maple syrup, rice wine vinegar, miso and 500ml hot vegetable stock, bring to the boil, then reduce to a simmer and cook for about 30 minutes until the carrots are tender. Blitz with a stick blender until smooth or blitz in a blender. Taste and season some more if needed. Put to one side until ready to serve. Serve hot!

3. For the vegetables, place the flour, egg and breadcrumbs on separate plates. Toss the vegetables in the flour, then the egg, then coat in the breadcrumbs. Heat 1 tablespoon of the olive oil in a non-stick frying pan and add some of the vegetables, but don't overcrowd the pan. Cook for 5–6 minutes, turning until golden and tender. Repeat, using more oil as you go, until all cooked. Serve as in the slow-cooker recipe.

Veggie sausage and beans in spicy tomato sauce with baked eggs, feta and coriander

(page 50)

SERVES 4
PREP 10 MINS
COOK 3 HOURS 15 MINS

1. Add the beans to a pan of water and cook for about 2 hours until the beans are tender. Drain well.

2. Heat the oil in a large, heavy-based pan, add the onion, season well and cook for a couple of minutes, then stir in the garlic and cook for a minute more. Stir in the paprika, chilli flakes and mustard, then add the tamarind pulp to 500ml hot vegetable stock and stir until dissolved. Pour it over the onion mix, then tip in the tomatoes, cooked beans and sausages and stir in the maple syrup. Bring to the boil, then reduce to a simmer and cook for about 1 hour, topping up with hot water if it needs it.

3. Make four indents in the pan, crack an egg into each one, put the lid on and cook for about 5 minutes or so until the eggs are cooked through. Top with feta and coriander to serve.

Courgette, pea, red pepper and goat's cheese frittata

(page 53)

SERVES 4
PREP 15 MINS
COOK 40 MINS

1. Preheat the oven to 190°C /170°C fan/ gas 5. Heat the oil in a large, non-stick frying pan. Add the onion, season well and cook for a couple of minutes, then stir in the garlic and cook for a minute more.

2. Add the courgettes and cook for about 5–6 minutes, stirring occasionally so they don't catch, then add the peppers and cook for a further 5 minutes or until soft.

3. Mix together the eggs, peas, goat's cheese, chives and mint, then pour them over the vegetable mix. Give the pan a shake so it is all even, cook gently for about 5 minutes, then put the pan in the oven (you may need to wrap foil around the handle) and cook for about 15–20 minutes, until the egg is just set. Remove from the oven (be careful – the handle will be hot), let it sit for 5 minutes, then slice and serve.

Red Thai tofu curry

(page 54)

SERVES 4
PREP 20 MINS
COOK 1 HOUR 25 MINS

1. Heat the oil in a large, deep pan, add the shallots, season well and cook for a few minutes. Stir in the garlic, ginger, chilli and lemongrass and cook for a few more minutes until everything is softened.

2. Stir in the Gochujang paste, tomato purée, soy sauce, lime juice and spices, stir well, then add the sugar, Thai basil leaves, cherry tomatoes, 500ml hot vegetable stock and coconut milk. Bring to a gentle boil, then reduce it to a simmer and cook for about an hour until the sauce has reduced and is full of flavour. If it needs topping up with hot water, do so, but be careful not to over dilute it.

3. Add the baby sweetcorn and sugar snap peas and cook for about 15 minutes until tender.

4. To cook the tofu, heat 1 tablespoon of the vegetable oil in a frying pan, add the tofu (you may have to do this in batches) and cook for several minutes, turning occasionally until golden. Top up with more oil as needed. Stir the spinach into the curry and, when wilted, add the tofu. Taste and adjust, as needed, the seasoning, lime juice, sugar and soy. Garnish with coriander and Thai basil leaves to serve.

Fresh & Fragrant

Smoky peppers and potatoes with toasted almonds *(page 58)*

SERVES 4
PREP 15 MINS
COOK 1 HOUR 10 MINS

1. First, cook the potatoes. Add them to a pan of salted water, bring to the boil, then reduce to a simmer and cook for about 15–20 minutes until almost tender, draining really well.

2. Heat the olive oil in a large, heavy-based pan, add the onion and thyme, season well and cook for a few minutes until softened. Add the garlic, both types of peppers, potatoes and paprika and turn to combine.

3. Cook over a medium heat, stirring occasionally and adding more oil as it needs it. Cook for about 15–20 minutes or until the peppers are tender.

4. Toast the almonds in a frying pan until pale golden, then roughly chop. Scatter them over the peppers along with the feta, garnish with thyme leaves and serve with French bread.

5. Alternatively, put the potatoes, peppers, thyme and roughly chopped onion in a large roasting tin, drizzle over the olive oil, add the paprika and season well. Toss to combine and bake in the oven at 200°C/180°C fan/gas 6 for about 1 hour until golden and beginning to char. Stir through the garlic and cook for a few minutes more. Top with the toasted almonds and feta as above and garnish with thyme leaves.

Slow-cooked cherry tomatoes with garlic

(page 61)

SERVES 4
PREP 5 MINS
COOK 2 HOURS

1. Preheat the oven to 180°C/160°C fan/gas 4. Put the tomatoes in a large roasting tin along with about 3 tablespoons olive oil. Season well, then combine everything together using your hands.

2. Put in the oven and slow roast for about 2 hours, adding the garlic for the last 1 hour of cooking. Check on them every now and then, adding a little more oil and giving them a gentle nudge around the tin if they are beginning to char too much or turning the oven down a little. Be careful as you don't want the garlic to burn as it will become bitter.

3. Remove from oven. Stir in the basil and serve as required, garnished with the whole basil leaves, or allow the sauce to go cold and keep in the fridge to use in a variety of different dishes.

Chunky Spanish stew

(page 62)

SERVES 4–6
PREP 20 MINS
COOK 1 HOUR 45 MINS

1. Preheat the oven to 190°C/170°C fan/gas 5. Heat the oil in a large, ovenproof pan, add the onion, season well and cook for a couple of minutes, then stir in the garlic and cook for a minute more.

2. Stir in the saffron and paprika spices, then add the sherry and sherry vinegar and bring to the bubble. Cook for a couple of minutes, then add the potatoes, peppers and thyme and stir so everything gets coated.

3. Pour in the passata and 700ml vegetable stock and add the sultanas and pine nuts. Bring to the boil, then remove from the heat, put the lid on and bake in the oven for 1–1½ hours, topping up with a little hot water if it starts to dry out at all. Serve as in the slow-cooker recipe.

Aubergine makhani

(page 65)

SERVES 4
PREP 10 MINS
COOK 1 HOUR 15 MINS

1. Heat the olive oil in a large, heavy-based pan, add the onion, season and cook for a few minutes, then stir in the garlic, chilli and ginger and cook for a minute more. Add the spices and curry leaves, stir well to combine, and cook for a couple of minutes. Don't allow anything to burn.

2. Add the aubergine and butter and stir to combine so the aubergine gets really well coated. Tip in the tomatoes, almonds and 300ml hot water, bring to the boil, then reduce to a simmer and cook for about 1 hour or until the aubergines are nice and tender. Top up with hot water as it needs it.

3. Stir in the cream and simmer for a few minutes, then stir in the coriander, taste and season some more if needed. Garnish with coriander leaves. Serve as in the slow-cooker recipe.

Courgette and tomato Provençal tian topped with goat's cheese

(page 66)

SERVES 4
PREP 25 MINS
COOK 50 MINS

1. Preheat the oven to 180°C/160°C fan/gas 4. Heat the oil in a frying pan, add the onion, season well and cook for a few minutes until softened, then stir in the garlic and cook for a minute more.

2. In an oiled ovenproof dish, about 20cm round, arrange the courgette, potato and tomato, alternating the colours in a circular arrangement and adding the onion, garlic, sumac, oregano and thyme in between. Drizzle over a little olive oil, season again, cover with foil and cook in the oven for about 30–40 minutes or until the potatoes are tender. Remove the foil for the last 15 minutes of cooking.

3. Sprinkle with the goat's cheese while it is hot so it melts into the mix. Garnish with fresh thyme and a drizzle of balsamic vinegar, if using. Serve with a rocket salad.

Slow-cooked BBQ jackfruit with slaw

(page 69)

SERVES 4–6
PREP 20 MINS
COOK 50 MINS

1. Heat the olive oil in a large, deep, heavy-based pan, add the onion, season well and cook for a couple of minutes, then stir in the garlic and cook for a minute more.

2. Stir in the passata, ketchup, vinegar, sugar, chilli flakes, soy sauce, paprika and mustard and add the jackfruit. Bring it to the boil, then reduce to a simmer and cook gently for about 40 minutes, topping up with hot water as it needs it. Separate the jackfruit using forks to shred it and stir it through the sauce. Taste and season as needed.

3. Serve the BBQ jackfruit along with the slaw and flatbreads.

Aubergine and tomato stew *(page 70)*

SERVES 4
PREP 20 MINS
COOK 55 MINS

1. Pour 1 tablespoon olive oil into a large, heavy-based pan, add the red onion and celery, season well and cook for a couple of minutes, then stir in the garlic, oregano and fennel seeds and cook for a minute more.

2. Add the remaining oil with the aubergines, stirring to combine, then cook over a slow heat, topping up with more oil as you need it. They will soak up the oil quite quickly. Cook until just beginning to soften and slightly char, then add the tomatoes and 250ml hot water mixed with the miso.

3. Bring the stew to the boil, then reduce to a simmer and cook for about 40–50 minutes, stirring occasionally and topping up with a little hot water if needed. Add the olives for the last 20 minutes of cooking. Taste and season some more if needed. Serve as in the slow-cooker recipe.

Vietnamese tofu pot with basil and mint

(page 73)

SERVES 4
PREP 20 MINS
COOK 1 HOUR 40 MINS

1. Heat the olive oil in a large, heavy-based pan, add the shallots and season well, cooking for a few minutes until the shallots are beginning to turn golden. Stir in the garlic, coriander seeds and star anise and cook for a minute more.

2. Add the ginger, chilli and lemongrass, pour over 900ml hot mushroom or vegetable stock and bring to the boil, then simmer gently for about 1 hour. You may need to top up with a little more hot water. To intensify the flavour, add a splash of dark soy sauce.

3. To cook the tofu, heat 1 tablespoon of the vegetable oil in a frying pan, add the tofu (you may have to do this in batches) and cook for several minutes, turning occasionally until golden. Top up with more oil as needed. Set to one side.

4. Add the carrots and mushrooms to the pan and cook for a further 30 minutes or until the carrots are tender. Add the sugar snap peas for the last 10 minutes of cooking. Taste and adjust the seasoning as needed. Add the tofu, top with the fresh herbs and garnish with the sliced chilli and lime wedges, if using.

Caribbean sunshine stew with mango *(page 74)*

SERVES 4
PREP 20 MINS
COOK 1 HOUR 10 MINS

1. Heat the oil in a large, heavy-based pan, add the onion and season well, cook for a couple of minutes, then stir in the garlic and spices and cook for a few minutes more.

2. Now stir in the tomatoes, peppers and sweet potato and give it a stir to combine, then add the chilli, beans, thyme leaves and mango pieces. Pour over 700ml hot vegetable stock, bring it to the boil, then reduce to a simmer and cook for about 50 minutes–1 hour until the veg is tender and the flavours have all melded together. Top up with more hot water as it cooks if needed and taste and season as required.

3. Serve the stew on its own or with rice, topped with thyme leaves and fresh mango pieces.

Summer vegetables *au vin* topped with gherkins *(page 77)*

SERVES 4
PREP 20 MINS
COOK 30 MINS

1. Heat the oil in a large, heavy-based pan, add the onion, season well and cook for a couple of minutes, then stir through the garlic and cook for a further minute.

2. Add the thyme, leeks, beans and courgettes and cook, stirring occasionally, for 4–5 minutes, then stir through the mustard and add the wine. Turn the heat up and let the wine bubble for a few minutes, then pour over 300ml hot vegetable stock. Bring it to the boil, then reduce to a simmer and cook for 10 minutes. Stir in the cream and continue to simmer gently for a further 10 minutes or until the vegetables are tender.

3. Stir through the spinach and taste and season some more as needed. Serve topped with cornichons, with bread on the side.

Stuffed aubergines with fresh tomato and parsley *(page 78)*

SERVES 4
PREP 15 MINS
COOK 1 HOUR 45 MINS

1. Preheat the oven to 200°C/180°C fan/gas 6. Heat 1 tablespoon of the oil in a large, heavy-based pan, add the onion, season well and cook for a couple of minutes, then stir through the garlic and chilli and cook for a further minute. Add the aubergine flesh, tomato and lemon juice and cook for 5 minutes, chopping it a little with the side of a wooden spoon. Stir in the chickpeas and parsley.

2. Drizzle a little olive oil into a large roasting tin. Sit the aubergine halves in the tin and spoon the mixture into each one.

3. Cover them with foil and cook in the oven for 1–1½ hours or until soft. Serve as in the slow-cooker recipe.

Korean spicy sauce with pak choi and noodles *(page 81)*

SERVES 4
PREP 15 MINS
COOK 25 MINS

1. First, lightly steam the pak choi. Sit it in a steamer or metal colander sat over a pan of just simmering water. Put a lid on and let it cook for about 5–6 minutes until just tender. Remove and put to one side.

2. Heat the sesame oil in a large frying pan or wok, add the spring onions and ginger, season well and stir-fry over a fairly high heat for a few minutes. Add the celery and continue to cook for a few more minutes, then add the garlic, moving it around the pan and being careful that the garlic doesn't burn.

3. Mix together the red wine vinegar, demerara sugar, soy and gochujang paste, add it to the pan and let it bubble for a few minutes. Add the mushroom or vegetable stock and continue to let it bubble, then throw in the tomatoes and stir. When the sauce has thickened, taste and season as needed, then throw in the noodles and coriander. Stir well to coat and heat through, then add the pak choi and top with sesame seeds to serve.

Indonesian-style summer rice pot *(page 82)*

SERVES 6–8
PREP 15 MINS
COOK 40 MINS

1. First, cook the rice. Put it in a pan and cover with water or vegetable stock so it sits about 5cm above the rice. Add a pinch of salt and cook with the lid on for about 15 minutes until the rice is tender. Remove from the heat, fluff up with a fork and put to one side (this recipe works better if the rice is cooked ahead and cooled completely before using).

2. Heat the oil in a large, deep frying pan or wok, add the onion, season well and cook for a couple of minutes, then stir in the garlic, ginger and chilli and cook for a couple of minutes more.

3. Add the courgette and peppers and stir around the pan for 6–8 minutes until they soften and cook. Stir in the kecap manis, soy sauce, sugar, lime juice and rice wine vinegar, let it bubble for a minute, then add the rice and stir everything together. Finally, stir in the sweetcorn and some of the pineapple. Cook until the rice is piping hot, taste and season some more if needed.

4. Serve with the toppings as in the slow-cooker recipe.

Superfood rice, grain and bean pot with nori seaweed and avocado

(page 85)

SERVES 4–6
PREP 5 MINS
COOK 30 MINS

1. First, cook the rice. Put it in a pan and cover with about 600ml water or vegetable stock so it sits a few centimetres above the rice. Add a pinch of salt and cook with the lid on for about 10–15 minutes until the rice is tender and has absorbed all the water. Remove from the heat and let the rice sit in the pan with the lid on for 5–10 minutes, then fluff it up with a fork.

2. Heat the olive oil in a large, deep frying pan, add the spring onion, season well and cook it for a couple of minutes, then stir in the garlic and ginger and cook for a couple of minutes more.

3. Stir in the chickpeas and flaxseeds, then tip in the rice and stir well to combine. Add the nori seaweed and sea salt mix and the chilli flakes. Taste and season some more if needed. Serve topped with pumpkin seeds and avocado and the lime wedges.

Butter beans in harissa and tahini sauce with dill and preserved lemon *(page 86)*

SERVES 4
PREP 10 MINS, PLUS OVERNIGHT SOAKING
COOK 3 HOURS

1. Soak the butter beans overnight and drain. Transfer them to a large pan and cover with water. Bring to the boil, then reduce to a high simmer, with the lid ajar, and cook for about 2 hours or until the butter beans are tender. Drain well and rinse. Put to one side.

2. Heat the oil in a large, deep, heavy-based pan, add the onion, season well and cook for a couple of minutes. Stir in the garlic, sumac and mint and cook for a further minute.

3. Stir in the beans and harissa, then tip in the preserved lemon, tomatoes, half the dill and 200ml hot water. Bring to the boil, then reduce to a simmer and cook for about 40 minutes until the sauce is beginning to reduce. Stir through the tahini and cook for a further 15 minutes, topping up with more hot water if it needs it. Taste and season if

required. Garnish with the remaining dill and pomegranate seeds, if using, and serve with the lemon wedges and bulgur wheat or couscous.

Tip: *Soaking the beans before cooking allows the beans to absorb water, which will start to dissolve the starches. It's the starches that can cause digestive discomfort, so it's an essential part of the process.*

Sweetcorn chowder

(page 89)

SERVES 4–6
PREP 20 MINS
COOK 40 MINS

1. Heat the olive oil with the butter in a large, heavy-based pan, add the onion, season well and cook for a couple of minutes, then stir in the garlic and cumin. Cook for a further minute.

2. Add the potatoes to the pan and stir until coated, then add the sweetcorn and pour in 500ml hot vegetable stock. Bring to the boil, then reduce to a simmer and cook for about 20–30 minutes or until the potatoes are tender. Top up with more hot water if needed.

3. Add the milk, cream and lots of black pepper and warm through. Blitz until almost smooth, leaving a little texture, then taste and season some more if needed. Serve with a drizzle of cream and garnish with watercress.

Greek-style stuffed peppers with rice and tomatoes (page 90)

SERVES 4
PREP 10 MINS
COOK 1¾–2¼ HOURS

1. Preheat the oven to 180°C/160°C fan/gas 4. Heat 1 tablespoon of the olive oil in a frying pan, add the red onion, season well and cook for a couple of minutes, then stir through the garlic, oregano, celery and chilli flakes and cook, stirring occasionally, for a few more minutes. Stir through the rice and sugar until the rice is really well coated.

2. Tip in the passata and stir well. Smother the peppers inside and out with the remaining olive oil, lightly oil a roasting tin and sit the peppers in it.

3. Divide the mixture among the peppers, then sit the tops on each one. Cover the roasting tin with foil, put it in the oven and cook for 1½–2 hours. Remove the foil and check to see if the rice is fully cooked. If it needs a little longer, tip a drizzle of hot water from the kettle into each pepper and let them continue cooking until the rice is tender. Remove and serve with a rocket and tomato salad.

Provençal green beans, olive and tomato (page 93)

SERVES 4
PREP 10 MINS
COOK 35 MINS

1. Put the green beans in a pan of boiling salted water and cook for about 5–6 minutes or until just tender. Drain, refresh with cold water and put to one side.

2. Heat half the olive oil in a large, deep frying pan, add the onion, season well and cook for a couple of minutes, then add the garlic and cook for a minute more.

3. Stir in the spices and the vinegar, let it bubble for 4–5 minutes until it has almost evaporated, then add the tomatoes and let them cook, squashing them with the back of a fork as they begin to soften. Add the remaining oil if needed, stir in the olives and add the green beans. Stir again so everything gets well coated and leave it to cook on low for 5–8 minutes for all the flavours to meld together. Taste and season some more if needed. Serve as in the slow-cooker recipe.

Sticky Japanese sauce with vegetables and noodles *(page 94)*

SERVES 4
PREP 15 MINS, PLUS 30 MINS PICKLING
COOK 30 MINS

1. Heat the sesame oil in a large frying pan or wok, add the sweetcorn, broccoli and green beans and season well. Now stir-fry on a high(ish) heat, moving them around the pan for 5–6 minutes.

2. Add the garlic, ginger and spring onions and stir-fry for a couple more minutes. Mix the rest of the sauce ingredients together, push the vegetables to one side and pour in, letting it bubble for a good 5–8 minutes.

3. Add the noodles to a large bowl, pour over hot water and leave for 2 minutes or as per the pack instructions, then drain well. Add them to the pan and stir everything together until all coated. Top with spring onion tops and the pickled radish, if using.

Sweet pepper and pea paneer curry *(page 97)*

SERVES 4–6
PREP 15 MINS
COOK 1 HOUR 40 MINS

1. Heat the oil in a large, heavy-based pan, add the onion, season well and cook for a couple of minutes, then stir in the garlic and chilli and cook for a minute more.

2. Add the peppers and stir so everything gets well coated. Pour in 700ml of the hot stock mixture, bring to a boil, then reduce to a simmer and cook for about an hour until the sauce has reduced down and the flavours have mingled, topping up with a little hot water if needed.

3. Add the paneer and cook for a further 30 minutes, then stir in the peas and coriander, taste and season as needed. Serve as in the slow-cooker recipe.

Comforting & Earthy

Miso ramen with mushrooms, pickled red cabbage and soy-soaked eggs *(page 103)*

SERVES 4
PREP 20 MINS
COOK 1 HOUR 45 MINS

1. Preheat the oven to 200°C/180°C fan/gas 6. Put the butternut squash in a large roasting tin, drizzle over 1 tablespoon olive oil (instead of the sesame oil), season and bake in the oven for about 30–40 minutes until tender and beginning to caramelise. Remove and put to one side. Prepare the soy eggs and red cabbage as in the slow-cooker recipe.

2. Put the miso in a large, deep pan, pour over 900ml hot vegetable stock, heat gently and stir until the miso dissolves. Stir in the soy sauce, mirin, spring onion, garlic, ginger and chilli. Bring to the boil, then reduce to a simmer and cook gently with the lid ajar for about 1–1½ hours, topping up with a little hot water if needed but being careful not to dilute the flavour too much. Stir through the noodles, porcini mushrooms and butternut squash and heat through. Adjust the flavour as needed with seasoning and soy sauce.

3. Serve with the toppings as in the slow-cooker recipe.

Pumpkin, chestnuts, green chilli and cinnamon stew *(page 104)*

SERVES 4
PREP 15 MINS
COOK 2 HOURS

1. Heat the olive oil in a large, heavy-based pan, add the onion, season well and cook for a couple of minutes, then add the garlic and chilli and cook for a minute more.

2. Stir in the cinnamon, chestnuts, pumpkin or squash, sage leaves, bay leaf and chilli flakes, if using, add the pearl barley and give it a good stir so everything gets well coated.

3. Pour in the passata and 700ml hot vegetable stock, stir again, bring it to the boil, then reduce to a simmer and cook for about 1–1½ hours or until the pumpkin or squash is tender, the pearl barley is cooked and the sauce has thickened. You may have to top it up with hot water as it cooks if it begins to dry out too much. Taste and season some more if needed. Serve as in the slow-cooker recipe.

Marrow and jackfruit casserole with cider, baby onions and apple

(page 107)

SERVES 4–6
PREP 20 MINS
COOK 2 HOURS 15 MINS

1. Preheat the oven to 200°C/180°C fan/gas 6. Heat the olive oil in a large, ovenproof, heavy-based pan, add the baby onions, season well and cook for about 5 minutes until beginning to soften. Stir in the garlic, thyme leaves, chilli flakes, paprika and oregano. Cook for 1 minute, then add the marrow and cook for a minute more. Pour in the cider and let it bubble for a couple of minutes, then add the apple, tomatoes and 500ml hot vegetable stock.

2. Bring to the boil, then reduce to a simmer, put a lid on and cook in the oven for about 1⅔–2 hours or until the marrow is tender. Top up with more hot water if it starts to dry out at all. Stir through the jackfruit for the last 30 minutes of cooking. Serve as in the slow-cooker recipe, with the topping if making.

Lentil and garlic stew topped with chilli oil

(page 108)

SERVES 4–6
PREP 20 MINS
COOK 1 HOUR 45 MINS

1. In a large, heavy-based pan, heat the oil, add the onion, carrot and celery, season well and cook for about 10 minutes until beginning to soften. Stir through the garlic and cook for a minute more.

2. Add the remaining ingredients, except the Parmesan and chilli oil or flakes, increasing the vegetable stock to 700ml, then stir really well so the lentils get well coated.

3. Bring it to the boil, then reduce to a simmer, put a lid on ajar and cook for about 1½ hours, stirring occasionally and checking that it is not drying out at all. Top up with hot water as it needs it. Taste and season as needed, then serve as in the slow-cooker recipe.

Cauliflower cheese soup with pickled walnuts *(page 111)*

SERVES 6
PREP 15 MINS
COOK 35 MINS

1. Pour the oil into a large, heavy-based pan, add the onion, season well and cook for a few minutes, then stir in the garlic and cook for a minute more.

2. Stir in the cauliflower and potato, mustard, nutmeg and 700ml vegetable stock, bring to the boil, then reduce to a simmer and cook for about 20–30 minutes or until the potato and cauliflower are tender. If it needs a little more stock, add it now.

3. Blitz with a stick blender until smooth, then stir through most of the cheese, reserving a little for the top. Serve as in the slow-cooker recipe.

Lentils and veggie sausages in romesco-style sauce

(page 112)

SERVES 4–6
PREP 20 MINS
COOK 2 HOURS 30 MINS

1. Preheat the oven to 200°C/180°C fan/gas 6. First, make the sauce. Put the peppers in a roasting tin, drizzle over the oil and bake in the oven for about 30 minutes or until tender and beginning to just blacken. Remove and transfer them to a blender along with the onion, garlic, sherry vinegar, smoked paprika, chilli and almonds and blitz until smooth. Reduce the oven to 190°C/170°C fan/gas 5.

2. Transfer the sauce to a large, ovenproof pan, stir in the lentils, 600ml hot vegetable stock and the veggie sausages. Put a lid on and bake in the oven for about 1½–2 hours or until the lentils are tender. Top up with a little hot water from the kettle if it begins to dry out at all. Taste and season as needed.

Moussaka *(page 115)*

SERVES 4–6
PREP 20 MINS
COOK 2 HOURS

1. First, cook the lentils. Add them to a pan of hot stock to cover, bring to the boil, then simmer for about 45–50 minutes until tender. Top up with more hot water as needed. Put to one side.

2. Brush each aubergine slice with olive oil, add to a non-stick frying pan, a few at a time, and cook until really golden on each side, adding more oil as you go. Put to one side.

3. Heat 1 tablespoon olive oil in the frying pan, add the onion, season well and cook for a few minutes, then stir in the garlic and cook for a minute more. Stir through the cinnamon, half the oregano and the nutmeg. Add the cooked lentils, passata and 200ml hot vegetable stock, stir and simmer for 10–15 minutes.

4. Add the potato slices to a pan of salted water and cook for about 15 minutes until just tender, then drain and put to one side.

5. Preheat the oven to 190°C/170°C fan/gas 5. To assemble, drizzle 1 tablespoon olive oil into a large, ovenproof dish. Layer with the potato, lentil mixture and aubergine, ending with a topping of potato.

6. Mix together the yoghurt, eggs and remaining oregano and pour over the top. Cover with foil and bake in the oven for about 30 minutes until piping hot, then remove the foil and cook for a further 10 minutes until golden. Serve as in the slow-cooker recipe.

Chunky 'roots' soup

(page 116)

SERVES 4
PREP 20 MINS
COOK 1 HOUR 15 MINS

1. Heat the oil in a large, heavy-based pan, add the onion, season well and cook for a few minutes until beginning to soften, add the garlic and bay leaf and cook for a minute more, then stir in the curry powder.

2. Add the sweet potatoes, carrots, parsnips, tomato purée and mustard and stir well so everything gets coated, then stir in the lentils and stock. Bring to the boil, then reduce to a simmer and cook with the lid ajar for about 1 hour or until the vegetables are tender. Top up with hot water if needed.

3. Stir in the butter beans and warm through, then serve as in the slow-cooker recipe.

Squash, mushroom and spinach lasagne *(page 119)*

SERVES 4–6
PREP 20 MINS
COOK 1 HOUR 50 MINS

1. Preheat the oven to 190°C/170°C fan/gas 5. Put the squash in a roasting tin, toss with 1 tablespoon olive oil, season and sprinkle with nutmeg and chilli flakes. Bake in the oven for about 40 minutes or until tender, then stir through the spinach – it should wilt in the heat. Put to one side.

2. Heat 1 tablespoon olive oil in a frying pan, add the mushrooms, season and cook for a few minutes until beginning to soften, then stir them in with the squash and spinach.

3. Heat another tablespoon olive oil in a large, deep frying pan, add the onion, season well and cook for a minute, then stir through the garlic and oregano and cook for a minute more. Stir in the passata and pesto and simmer gently for about 10 minutes.

4. Layer the lasagne in a large, ovenproof dish, starting with the tomato sauce, then the squash mixture, followed by the ricotta, mozzarella and lasagne sheets and ending with the tomato sauce. Top with Parmesan, cover the dish with foil and bake in the oven for about 40 minutes or until the pasta is tender when poked with a sharp knife. Remove the foil and cook for 10 minutes more for the top to brown. Serve with a rocket salad.

Chickpea balls in tomato sauce *(page 120)*

SERVES 4
PREP 20 MINS
COOK 2 HOURS

1. Heat 1 tablespoon oil in a frying pan, add the onion, season well and cook for a minute, then add the garlic and sage leaves and cook for a minute more. Transfer half to a food processor (reserve half for the sauce) along with the chickpeas, walnut halves, breadcrumbs, oregano, paprika and miso and pulse until combined. Give it a taste before you combine with the egg, and season some more if needed. Pulse until it comes together and roll into 16 balls.

2. Heat 1 tablespoon olive oil in a large, non-stick frying pan, add the balls and fry for about 3–4 minutes each side until golden. You may need to do a few at a time, and you will need to add more oil as you go. Preheat the oven to 190°C/170°C fan/gas 5.

3. Tip the reserved onion mix into a large, heavy-based, ovenproof pan, add the passata, chilli flakes, capers and 200ml hot vegetable stock. Add the balls to the sauce, pushing them down so they are almost covered, put a lid on and bake in the oven for 1–1½ hours. Top up with a little hot water if it dries out too much.

Black bean and squash stew with chipotle and sour cream drizzle

(page 123)

SERVES 6
PREP 15 MINS, PLUS OVERNIGHT SOAKING
COOK 4 HOURS 30 MINS

1. Soak the black beans overnight. Rinse them well, then add them to a large pan of salted water. Bring to the boil, then reduce to a simmer and cook for 1–2 hours until tender. Remove any scum and drain well.

2. Preheat the oven to 190°C/170°C fan/gas 5. Heat the oil in a large, heavy-based, ovenproof pan, add the onion, season well and cook for a few minutes, then add the garlic and chilli and cook for a minute more. Stir in the herbs and spices, cook for a few seconds, then stir in the squash, beans, tomatoes and 3 tins of water and the lime juice. Stir, put the lid on and bake in the oven for 1½–2 hours, topping up with hot water as it starts to dry out.

3. Taste and season some more if needed. Stir through the coriander and serve as in the slow-cooker recipe.

Persian-style veggie mince *(page 124)*

SERVES 4
PREP 10 MINS
COOK 1 HOUR

1. Heat the oil in a frying pan, add the onion, season well and cook for a few minutes, then add the garlic and cook for a minute more. Stir in the turmeric, cumin, cinnamon, sumac and pul biber or chilli flakes.

2. Add the veg mince, walnuts, apricots, tomato purée and stock.

3. Stir well, bring to a boil, then reduce to a simmer and cook gently, stirring occasionally, for about 40 minutes, topping up with hot water if it needs it.

4. Stir through the coriander, taste and season some more if required. Serve as in the slow-cooker recipe.

Polish pickle soup

(page 127)

SERVES 4–6
PREP 20 MINS
COOK 1 HOUR 45 MINS

1. Heat the oil in a large, heavy-based pan, add the onion, season well and cook for a couple of minutes, then add the garlic and celery and cook for 6–8 minutes until beginning to soften.

2. Stir in the carrots, gherkins, potatoes, dill and cabbage and stir well so everything gets coated. Pour over the stock, bring to the boil, then reduce to a simmer and cook for 1–1½ hours until all the vegetables are tender, topping up with hot water if needed.

3. Stir through the sour cream for the last 15 minutes of cooking. Taste and season some more if needed. Garnish with the reserved dill before serving.

Vegetable goulash

(page 128)

SERVES 4
PREP 20 MINS
COOK 2 HOURS

1. Heat the oil in a large, heavy-based pan, add the onion, season well and cook for a minute, then stir in the garlic and bay leaf and cook for a further minute. Stir in the caraway and paprika spices and cook for a few seconds.

2. Add the potatoes, parsnips, mushrooms, tomatoes, tomato purée, mustard and 700ml mushroom or vegetable stock, stir well and bring to the boil. Sit the lid ajar and reduce to a simmer, then cook for about 1–1¼ hours or until the vegetables are tender. Top up with a little hot water if needed.

3. Serve as in the slow-cooker recipe.

'Faux duck' hoisin

(page 131)

SERVES 4
PREP 15 MINS
COOK 40 MINS

1. Heat half the sesame oil in a deep frying pan and add the garlic. Cook for a few seconds to soften, then add all the other ingredients except the 'faux duck'. Bring to the boil, then reduce to a simmer, giving it a stir with a balloon whisk until smooth. Top up with a little more hot water if it needs it. Simmer until thickened and tasty.

2. In another frying pan, heat the remaining sesame oil, add the 'faux duck' and fry for about 10 minutes or as per the pack instructions.

3. To serve, spoon a little of the sauce down the middle of a warmed pancake or wrapper, top with the faux duck, cucumber and spring onion slices, roll and eat!

Mung bean and paneer curry *(page 132)*

SERVES 6
PREP 20 MINS, PLUS OVERNIGHT SOAKING
COOK 2 HOURS 15 MINS

1. Soak the mung beans overnight before using.

2. Heat the oil in a large, heavy-based deep pan, add the onion, season well and cook for a few minutes, then stir in the garlic, ginger and chilli and cook for a minute more. Add the turmeric, curry leaves, coriander seeds, cardamom seeds, cumin seeds and garam masala and cook for a few minutes.

3. Stir in the tomato purée, tomatoes and soaked and rinsed mung beans, then pour over the vegetable stock and add the cinnamon stick. Bring to the boil then, with the lid ajar, simmer for about 1 hour, topping up with hot water if it is starting to dry out at all.

4. Add the paneer and continue to simmer for a further 30–40 minutes until soft and the flavours have all mingled, adding more hot water if needed. Stir through the spinach and cook until it wilts, then add the lemon juice to taste. Serve as in the slow-cooker recipe.

Squash and potato dauphinoise *(page 135)*

SERVES 4–6
PREP 20 MINS
COOK 1 HOUR 30 MINS

1. Preheat the oven to 190°C/170°C fan/gas 5. Heat the oil in a large frying pan, add the onion, season well and cook for a minute, then stir in the nutmeg, garlic, sage and thyme and cook for a minute more.

2. Add the squash and potatoes, turn to coat, then transfer it all to a large ovenproof dish. Flatten the top and then pour over the cream.

3. Top with Gruyère, cover with foil and bake in the oven for about 1 hour, then remove the foil and cook for a further 15 minutes until turning golden and the potatoes and squash are tender.

Middle-Eastern chickpea stew *(page 136)*

SERVES 4–6
PREP 20 MINS, PLUS OVERNIGHT SOAKING
COOK 2 HOUR 45 MINS

1. Soak the chickpeas overnight, drain them well, rinse and add to a large pan of salted water. Bring to the boil, then reduce to a simmer and cook with the lid ajar for about 45 minutes. Remove any scum and drain well.

2. Preheat the oven to 190°C/170°C fan/gas 5. In a large, heavy-based, ovenproof pan, heat the oil, add the onion, season well and cook for a minute, then add the garlic and cook for a further minute. Stir in the ground spices and cook for a few seconds, then tip in the drained chickpeas.

3. Add the saffron and water and the leeks, swede, carrots and chilli flakes and stir around the pan to get coated with the spices. Add the maple syrup, passata and 700ml hot vegetable stock, bring to the boil, then reduce to a simmer, put a lid on and bake in the oven for about 1–1½ hours until the vegetables are tender, topping up with a little hot water if needed. Stir in the lemon juice and parsley and season some more if needed. Top with za'atar and serve as in the slow-cooker recipe.

Dried fruit pilaf *(page 139)*

SERVES 6
PREP 15 MINS
COOK 1 HOUR

1. Heat the oil in a large, heavy-based pan, add the onion, season well and cook for a couple of minutes, then stir through the garlic and chilli and cook for a minute more. Stir through the turmeric, cinnamon and nutmeg.

2. Tip in the rice and spelt, stir and add the stock, bring to the boil, then reduce to a simmer and cook for about 20–30 minutes, stirring occasionally and topping up with hot water if it starts to dry out at all.

3. Cook the cavolo nero or kale in a pan of salted water for about 15 minutes or until just tender, then drain well. Add the fruit and nuts to the rice mixture and stir well, then add the cooked cavolo nero or kale. Continue cooking on low and stirring until the rice is cooked and tender, then taste and season some more if needed. Serve as in the slow-cooker recipe.

Mushroom ragu with pappardelle *(page 140)*

SERVES 4–6
PREP 15 MINS
COOK 1 HOUR 30 MINS

1. Heat the oil in a large, heavy-based pan, add the onion, season well and cook for a few minutes, then add the garlic, celery and thyme and cook for about 10–15 minutes, stirring occasionally, until softened, making sure the garlic doesn't burn.

2. Add both kinds of mushrooms and cook for a further 10 minutes until they are beginning to reduce down, then stir in the tomato purée, mustard, capers, passata, 500ml hot vegetable stock and chilli flakes.

3. Cook for about an hour, breaking up the mushrooms with the side of a wooden spoon as the sauce cooks and absorbs all the liquid, topping up with more hot water if it needs it. Taste and season some more if needed.

4. Cook the pasta in a pan of boiling salted water for 6–8 minutes or as per the pack instructions and toss with the sauce.

Warming & Hearty

Beetroot, orange and rosemary soup with whipped feta *(page 145)*

SERVES 4–6
PREP 20 MINS
COOK 1 HOUR 40 MINS

1. Add the unpeeled whole beetroot to a large pan, cover with water and cook for about 1 hour or until tender when poked with a knife. Drain, then peel when cool enough to handle. Cut into chunky pieces.

2. Heat the oil in a large, heavy-based pan, add the onion and celery, season well and cook for a couple of minutes until softened, then stir in the garlic, chilli flakes and rosemary and cook for a minute more. Add the potatoes and beetroot and pour over the vegetable stock and orange juice. Bring to the boil, then reduce to a simmer and cook for about 30–40 minutes or until the potatoes are tender and the stock has reduced slightly.

3. Blitz the soup with a stick blender or transfer it to a blender and whizz until blended to your required consistency. Serve with the topping as in the slow-cooker recipe.

Tempeh stew with sherry vinegar, star anise and prunes *(page 146)*

SERVES 4
PREP 15 MINS
COOK 1 HOUR 45 MINS

1. Heat the oil in a large, deep, heavy-based pan, add the onion, season well and cook for a couple of minutes, then add the garlic, rosemary and tempeh and cook for about 5 minutes, stirring occasionally, until the tempeh is beginning to turn golden.

2. Turn the heat up, add the star anise and sherry vinegar and let it bubble for a few minutes, then stir in the carrots, leeks, tomato purée, mustard, prunes and a little of the vegetable stock and bring it to the boil. Add the remaining stock, put a lid on and bake it in the oven for about 1–1½ hours, checking to see it isn't drying out at all. If it is, top up with hot water.

3. Remove from the oven, taste and season some more if needed. Serve as in the slow-cooker recipe.

Portobello mushroom stew with dumplings

(page 149)

SERVES 4
PREP 20 MINS
COOK 2 HOURS 15 MINS

1. Preheat the oven to 190°C/170°C fan/gas 5. In a large, heavy-based, ovenproof dish, heat the oil, add the onion, celery and carrot, season well and cook for about 10 minutes or until beginning to soften, then stir in the garlic and cook for a minute more.

2. Stir in the potatoes, tomato purée, peanut butter, tamari or soy, paprika and thyme and stir well. Add a little of the mushroom or vegetable stock, bring it to the boil, then give it another stir and add the remaining stock. Put a lid on and bake in the oven for about 2 hours, checking that it doesn't dry out at all. Top up with a little hot water from the kettle if it needs it.

3. Prepare the dumplings by putting the flour in a large bowl and seasoning well, then rub the butter into the flour using your fingertips until it resembles breadcrumbs. Stir through

Continues overleaf >

the Parmesan. Slowly add the cold water a little at a time and begin to gently pull the mixture together to incorporate the water – when it's ready it should all come away from the side of the bowl. Try not to overhandle so that it remains light. Cut it into 12 equal pieces and roll into balls.

4. Add the dumplings to the stew along with the mushrooms for the last 30 minutes of cooking. The dumplings will rise to the top and spread out when they are cooked. Garnish with parsley leaves, if using, and serve as in the slow-cooker recipe.

Leek and pink peppercorn risotto with Shropshire Blue *(page 150)*

SERVES 4
PREP 10 MINS
COOK 35 MINS

1. Heat the oil and butter in a large, deep frying pan, add the onion, season well and cook for a few minutes, then stir in the garlic and cook for a further minute.

2. Add the leeks and pink peppercorns and cook, stirring occasionally, for 5–6 minutes until beginning to soften, then stir through the rice and turn until the rice is well coated. Pour in the wine and bubble for a few minutes, then begin to ladle in the hot vegetable stock a little at a time, stirring as you go (you may need a little more hot stock).

3. Continue to ladle and stir for about 20 minutes, until the rice is just tender and creamy, then remove from the heat and stir through the blue cheese, leaving a little for the topping. Serve as in the slow-cooker recipe.

Mac and cheese with butternut squash *(page 153)*

SERVES 4–6
PREP 15 MINS
COOK 1 HOUR 15 MINUTES

1. Preheat the oven to 200°C/180°C fan/gas 6. Put the squash in a large roasting tin, drizzle over the olive oil and season well. Bake in the oven for about 30–40 minutes until tender and golden. Put to one side. Turn the oven down to 190°C/170°C fan/gas 5.

2. Add the macaroni to a pan of boiling salted water and cook for about 12 minutes or as per the pack instructions until just tender, being careful to not overcook it. Drain well and put to one side.

3. Melt the butter in a pan, stir in 1 tablespoon plain flour and cook for a minute, then slowly stir in the milk and keep stirring and adding until it begins to thicken. Remove from the heat and stir in the mustard, cream cheese and grated cheese and season.

4. Combine the squash, macaroni and cheese sauce and transfer it to a large, ovenproof dish. Stir through the red onion. Cover with foil, put in the oven and bake for about 30 minutes or until piping hot. Remove the foil and let it cook a little longer until golden and crispy. Serve with the crispy sage leaves as in the slow-cooker recipe.

Leek and potato chunky soup with Stilton toasties *(page 154)*

SERVES 4–6
PREP 15 MINS
COOK 1 HOUR

1. Heat the oil in a large, heavy-based pan, add the onion, season well and cook for 2 minutes, then stir through the garlic and sage and cook for a minute more.

2. Add the leeks to the pan, cook for about 5 minutes until they are beginning to soften, then stir in the potatoes and cook for 5 minutes more, stirring occasionally so it doesn't catch. Add the cider, if using, turn the heat up and bubble for a minute, then add 900ml hot vegetable stock and let it bubble for a few more minutes.

3. Reduce to a simmer, stir in the mustard and cook gently with the lid ajar for about 45 minutes–1 hour, tasting and seasoning as needed. Serve with the Stilton toasties as in the slow-cooker recipe.

Parsnip and carrot tagine with ginger and rhubarb topping *(page 157)*

SERVES 4
PREP 20 MINS
COOK 1 HOUR 30 MINS

1. Preheat the oven to 190°C/170°C fan/gas 5. Prepare the rhubarb by putting the chopped rhubarb pieces and half the ginger in a small pan. Add about 1 tablespoon water and sweeten with a pinch of brown sugar, if wished. Simmer for a few minutes until tender, then put to one side.

2. In a bowl, mix together 1 tablespoon of the olive oil, the garlic, turmeric, remaining ginger, cumin, paprika, harissa and half the finely chopped parsley. Stir in 200ml water.

3. Heat the remaining oil in a large, ovenproof dish, add the onion, season well and cook for a couple of minutes, then add the spice mix and cook for a minute more. Tip in the tomatoes.

4. Now layer all the vegetables and the spice mixture, sit a lid on top and bake in the oven for about 1 hour or until the vegetables are tender. Top up with a little hot water if it starts to dry out at all. Stir through the olives and serve with the remaining parsley and the rhubarb topping as in the slow-cooker recipe.

Celeriac, tamarind and peanut stew with apple salsa *(page 158)*

SERVES 6–8
PREP 15 MINS
COOK 1 HOUR 45 MINS

1. Preheat the oven to 190°C/170°C fan/gas 5. Heat the oil in a deep, heavy-based, ovenproof pan, add the onion, season well and cook for a minute, then stir in the garlic, celery and thyme leaves and cook for a further few minutes.

2. Add the celeriac, tamarind, peanut butter, mustard and butter beans and stir, then pour in 900ml vegetable stock and bring to the boil. Reduce to a simmer, put a lid on and bake in the oven for about 1½ hours, until the veg is tender. Top up with hot water if needed. Stir through the spinach until it wilts.

3. Serve with the apple topping as in the slow-cooker recipe.

Jerusalem artichoke and potato stew with clementine and parsley gremolata topping

(page 161)

SERVES 4
PREP 20 MINS
COOK 1 HOUR 45 MINS

1. Preheat the oven to 190°C/170°C fan/gas 5. Heat the oil in a deep, heavy-based, ovenproof pan, add the onion, season well and cook for a minute, then add the oregano, rosemary and garlic and cook for a few more minutes.

2. Add the Jerusalem artichokes and potatoes and stir around the pan, then add the clementine peel and juice and the porcini

Continues overleaf >

mushrooms and reserved juice. Pour in 800ml hot mushroom or vegetable stock, bring to the boil, then reduce to a simmer, put the lid on and bake in the oven for 1–1½ hours or until the potatoes are tender. Top up with a little hot water if needed.

3. Serve with the clementine and parsley gremolata topping as in the slow-cooker recipe.

Irish stew *(page 162)*

SERVES 4–6
PREP 20 MINS
COOK 2 HOURS

1. Preheat the oven to 190°C/170°C fan/gas 5. Heat the oil in a large, heavy-based, ovenproof pan. Add the onion, season well and cook for a couple of minutes, then add the garlic, rosemary and celery and cook for a few minutes more.

2. Pour in the Guinness and let it bubble for a few minutes.

3. Add the potatoes, carrots, turnips, leeks, mushrooms, tomato purée, sugar, if using, and lentils and pour over 700ml hot vegetable stock.

4. Put the lid on and bake in the oven for 1–1½ hours or until all the vegetables are tender. Top up with hot water if it starts to dry out at all. Serve as in the slow-cooker recipe.

Portuguese-style potato and three greens soup *(page 165)*

SERVES 4–6
PREP 20 MINS
COOK 1 HOUR

1. Heat the oil in a large, heavy-based deep pan, add the onion, season well and cook for a couple of minutes, then add the garlic and cook for a minute more.

2. Add the potatoes, pouring in more oil as needed, and cook them, stirring occasionally so they don't stick, for about 5–6 minutes.

3. Turn the heat up, add a little of the vegetable stock and let it bubble for a few minutes, then add the remaining stock, bubble, then turn it down to a low simmer and cook for about 20 minutes until the potatoes are tender and the stock has reduced. Add all the greens and the chilli flakes and cook for a further 6–8 minutes or until the cabbage is just tender. Taste and season some more if needed. Serve as in the slow-cooker recipe.

Slow-cooked sprouts, red onion and garlic with a lemon and tahini dressing *(page 166)*

SERVES 4
PREP 20 MINS
COOK 45 MINS

1. Heat the oil in a large, heavy-based pan, add the onion, season well and cook for a few minutes until softened, then stir in the garlic and thyme and cook for a few minutes more, being careful not to burn the garlic.

2. Add the sprouts, miso and maple syrup and toss around the pan, adding a few drops of water. Stir and cook for about 15 minutes or until the sprouts are tender. Add a trickle more water if needed. Finally, add the flaked almonds.

3. Serve with the tahini and lemon dressing as in the slow-cooker recipe.

Red cabbage with ginger beer topped with dates and Stilton

(page 169)

SERVES 6
PREP 15 MINS
COOK 1 HOUR 45 MINS

1. Heat the oil in a large, heavy-based pan, add the onion, ginger, apple, cabbage and garlic, season well and cook, stirring occasionally, for 6–8 minutes.

2. Turn the heat up, pour in the ginger beer and vinegar and let it bubble for a few minutes, then reduce the heat to a low simmer and add the star anise, cinnamon stick, sultanas and sugar.

3. Cook with the lid ajar for 1–1½ hours until the cabbage is tender and sweet. Top up with a little hot water if it starts to dry out at all. Scatter over the dates and Stilton, if using.

Italian ribollita *(page 170)*

SERVES 4–6
PREP 15 MINS
COOK 1 HOUR 45 MINS

1. Heat the oil in a large, deep, heavy-based pan, add the onion, season well and cook for a minute, then stir in the garlic, chilli flakes and celery and cook for a few more minutes until the celery is beginning to soften.

2. Add the carrots, Parmesan rind or yeast flakes and beans, cavolo nero and 900ml hot vegetable stock with the tomato purée. Stir, bring to the boil, then reduce to a simmer and cook with the lid ajar for about 1–1½ hours or until the vegetables are tender. Top up with a little hot water from the kettle if needed. Serve as in the slow-cooker recipe.

Yellow split pea soup with yoghurt and toasted almonds *(page 173)*

SERVES 4–6
PREP 10 MINS
COOK 2 HOURS

1. Heat the oil in a large, heavy-based pan, add the onion, season well and cook for a few minutes until soft, then stir in the garlic and ginger and cook for a minute more.

2. Stir in the spices and cook for a few seconds, then stir in the split peas, passata and 900ml hot vegetable stock. Bring to the boil, then reduce to a simmer and cook with the lid ajar for about 1–1½ hours or until tender, topping up with a little hot water if it gets dry. Taste and season some more if needed. Serve as in the slow-cooker recipe.

Pottage pie *(page 174)*

SERVES 4
PREP 15 MINS
COOK 2 HOURS

1. Preheat the oven to 190°C/170°C fan/gas 5. Heat the oil in a large, heavy-based pan, add the onion, season well and cook for a minute, then add the garlic and celery and cook for a few minutes more until the celery is soft. Stir in the oregano, cinnamon and cumin and cook for a few seconds.

2. Stir in the lentils, carrot, tomato purée and yeast extract and cook for a few minutes, then pour in the vegetable stock, stir and bring to the boil. Reduce to a simmer and cook for about 45 minutes or until the lentils and carrots are tender. Top up with hot water if it needs it. Transfer to an ovenproof dish.

3. Top with the sweet potato, dot with butter, cover with foil and bake in the oven for 45 minutes–1 hour until the potato is tender. Remove the foil, top with the cheese and put back in the oven for 10 minutes or until the cheese is melted.

Black-eyed beans spicy pot with polenta dumplings *(page 177)*

SERVES 4–6
PREP 20 MINS, PLUS OVERNIGHT SOAKING
COOK 2 HOURS

1. Soak the beans overnight. Preheat the oven to 190°C/170°C fan/gas 5. Heat the oil in a large, heavy-based, ovenproof pan. Add the onion and spring onion, season well and cook for a minute, then add the garlic and chilli and cook for a minute more. Stir in the spices and cook for a few seconds.

2. Add the beans, tomatoes and 900ml vegetable stock. Bring to the boil, then reduce to a simmer. Put the lid on and bake in the oven for about 1½ hours until the beans are tender. Top up with hot water if needed.

3. To make the dumplings, put the flour and polenta in a bowl, season, add the cheese and egg and trickle in the milk. Stir gently and pull it all together until combined.

4. Add to the pot for the last ½ hour of cooking, spooning in about 12 dollops of the mixture to form the dumplings. Garnish with coriander, if using.

Kashmiri veggie mince curry with cucumber pickle *(page 178)*

SERVES 4–6
PREP 15 MINS
COOK 1 HOUR 15 MINS

1. Heat the oil in a deep, heavy-based pan, add the onion, season well and cook for a minute, then stir in the garlic, chilli and ginger and cook for a couple more minutes.

2. Stir through the ground spices and cook for a minute, then add the cinnamon stick, potatoes, tomatoes, plant mince, tomato purée and 800ml hot vegetable stock.

3. Bring to the boil, then reduce to a simmer and cook for about 1 hour or until the potatoes are tender, topping up with a little hot water from the kettle if it needs it. Taste and season some more if needed. To serve, stir through the lemon juice and coriander. Serve alongside cucumber pickle (see page 34).

Mulligatawny pot *(page 181)*

SERVES 4–6
PREP 15 MINS
COOK 1 HOUR 15 MINS

1. Heat the oil in a large, heavy-based pan, add the onion, season well and cook for a minute, then add the garlic, ginger, chilli and mustard seeds and cook for a minute more. Stir in the garam masala, curry powder and turmeric and cook for a few seconds.

2. Add the potato, parsnip, carrot, apple and lentils, stir well and pour over 900ml of the vegetable stock and tomato purée mixture. Bring to the boil, then reduce to a simmer and cook for about 1 hour or until the vegetables are tender, topping up with hot water if needed.

3. Stir through the mango chutney and lime juice, if using. Taste and season some more if needed, then garnish with coriander, if using.

Whole 'roast' cauliflower and root vegetables *(page 182)*

SERVES 4
PREP 15 MINS
COOK 1½ HOURS

1. Preheat the oven to 200°C/180°C fan/gas 6. Put the cauliflower, potato, onion, carrot, parsnip and garlic in a large roasting tin.

2. Add the thyme, season well, drizzle over the maple syrup and olive oil and dot with the butter. Bake in the oven for about 1–1½ hours or until everything is tender and golden. Cover with foil if it starts to brown too quickly.

Thanks

This book has been a joy to work on from beginning to end. I owe a really big thank you in the first instance to Daniel Hurst, the Cookery Publisher at Michael Joseph, Penguin Random House, for saying yes and agreeing to the idea of this book. I have had the idea of year-round vegetarian meals in the slow cooker 'stewing' for quite a long time!

A big thank you to Aggie Russell, Editor, who was a real pleasure to work with, and to William Shaw, photographer, who made every picture look delicious – being presented with a black pot of food on repeat is no mean feat. Shooting in my kitchen was done at such a relaxing and enjoyable pace with our small team of three. Thank you! And thank you to the words and pictures team back at the office, who bring the book to life – loving the layout and the cover. Thank you to Sarah Fraser, Head of Illustrated Books; Dan Prescott-Bennet, Designer; Gail Jones, Designer; Nikki Ellis, Designer; and Emma Henderson, Senior Editorial Manager.

I live in a household of mixed diets and ages: me, the vegetarian; husband and one grandson, meat-eaters; daughter, vegan; and second grandson, picky! As a cook I tend not to like gimmicky appliances or utensils, but the slow cooker has had a place in my kitchen for many years (I have three). The slow cooker is invaluable when everyone wants to eat at different times with different requirements, and I love to use it for batch cooking for the freezer. So, with my mixed bag of recipe testers at home, I've had some really helpful (and sometimes not so helpful) feedback, which has resulted in an eclectic list of recipes that I feel truly happy with – I really hope you enjoy cooking them too.

A huge thank you, as ever, to my husband Jos, who is always supportive of every project I'm involved in, and who never objects to the upheaval of photography shoots and recipe testing at home – and eating endless pots of the same food on repeat.

Index

a

apples
   celeriac, tamarind and peanut stew with apple salsa **158**
   marrow and jackfruit casserole with cider, baby onions and apple **107**

asparagus
   asparagus ends soup with soft boiled egg and cress topping **37**, **191**
   new potato and asparagus pot with goat's cheese **21**
   saffron rice with asparagus and dill raita **22**
   spring green minestrone with orzo pasta **30**

aubergines
   aubergine and tomato stew **70**, **196**
   aubergine makhani **66**, **197**
   Malaysian-style curry with sambal, aubergine and okra **34**
   moussaka stew **115**
   stuffed aubergines with fresh tomato and parsley **78**, **197**

avocados: superfood rice, grain and bean pot with nori seaweed and avocado **84**

b

basmati rice **14**

BBQ jackfruit with slaw **69**, **195**

beans
   black bean and squash stew with chipotle and sour cream drizzle **120**
   black eyed beans spicy pot with polenta dumplings **177**
   brown rice and soya pilaf in a sweet Asian sauce **38**
   butter beans in harissa and tahini sauce with dill and preserved lemon **86**
   Caribbean sunshine stew with mango **74**
   dried **7–8**
   Italian ribollita **170**
   mung bean and paneer curry **132**
   new potato and asparagus pot with goat's cheese **21**
   Provençal green beans, olive and tomato **93**
   sticky Japanese sauce with vegetables and noodles **94**
   summer vegetables *au vin* topped with gherkins **77**

beetroot, orange and rosemary soup with whipped feta **145**, **207**

black bean and squash stew with chipotle and sour cream drizzle **204**

black eyed beans spicy pot with polenta dumplings **177**, **212**

braised leeks, courgettes, spring carrots and tarragon with a mustard dressing **46**, **192**

bread: Mediterranean layered savoury bread-and-butter bake with feta **41**

broccoli
   spring veg katsu curry **49**
   sticky Japanese sauce with vegetables and noodles **94**

brown rice and soya pilaf in a sweet
    Asian sauce **38**

butter beans in harissa and tahini sauce **86**, **198**

c

cabbage

    miso ramen with mushrooms, pickled red
        cabbage and soy-soaked eggs **103**

    Portuguese-style potato a
        nd three greens soup **165**

    red cabbage with ginger beer topped
        with dates and Stilton **169**, **211**

    Singapore noodles with egg scramble **26**

    slow-cooked BBQ jackfruit with slaw **69**

    spring green minestrone with orzo pasta **30**

    sweet potato, spring cabbage and fennel pot
        with harissa and lemon **29**

Caribbean sunshine stew with mango **74**, **196**

carrots

    braised leeks, courgettes, spring carrots
        and tarragon with a mustard dressing **46**

    chunky 'roots' soup **116**

    Italian ribollita **170**

    Middle-Eastern chickpea stew **136**

    mulligatawny pot **181**

    parsnip and carrot tagine with ginger
        and rhubarb topping **157**

    Polish pickle soup **127**

    spring carrot and chives soup **45**

    Vietnamese tofu pot with basil and mint **73**

    whole 'roast' cauliflower and root
        vegetables **182**

cauliflower

    cauliflower cheese soup
        with pickled walnuts **111**, **202**

    parsnip and carrot tagine with ginger
        and rhubarb topping **157**

    whole 'roast' and root vegetables **182**

celeriac, tamarind and peanut stew
    with apple salsa **158**

cheese

    beetroot, orange and rosemary soup
        with whipped feta **145**

    cauliflower cheese soup with pickled walnuts **111**

    courgette, pea, red pepper
        and goat's cheese frittata **53**

    courgette and tomato Provençal tian topped
        with goat's cheese **61**

    leek and pink peppercorn risotto
        with Shropshire blue **150**

    leek and potato chunky soup
        with Stilton toasties **154**

    mac and cheese with butternut squash **153**

    Mediterranean layered savoury
        bread-and-butter bake with feta **41**

    new potato and asparagus pot
        with goat's cheese **21**

    pottage pie **174**

    red cabbage with ginger beer topped
        with dates and Stilton **169**

    veggie sausage and beans
        in spicy tomato sauce **50**

chestnuts: pumpkin, green chilli
    and cinnamon stew **104**

chickpeas

    chickpea balls in tomato sauce **120**, **203**

    Middle-Eastern chickpea stew **136**

    superfood rice, grain and bean pot
        with nori seaweed and avocado **84**

courgettes

    braised leeks, courgettes, spring carrots
        and tarragon with a mustard dressing **46**

courgette, pea, red pepper
    and goat's cheese frittata **53**
courgette and tomato Provençal tian topped
    with goat's cheese **61**, **195**
Indonesian-style summer rice pot **82**
pearl barley risotto with courgette and tomato **33**
spring veg katsu curry **49**
summer vegetables *au vin* topped
    with gherkins **77**

cucumber
    pickle **34**
    relish **178**

curries
    aubergine makhani **65**, **193**
    Kashmiri veggie mince curry
        with cucumber pickle **178**, **212**
    Malaysian-style curry with sambal,
        aubergine and okra **34**, **190**
    mung bean and paneer curry **132**, **205**
    red Thai tofu curry **54**, **193**
    spring veg katsu curry **49**, **192**
    sweet pepper and pea paneer curry **97**, **200**
    Thai green curry **25**, **189**

d

dressings
    lemon and tahini **166**
    mustard **46**
dried fruit pilaf **139**, **206**
dumplings
    black eyed beans spicy pot
        with polenta dumplings **177**
    portobello mushroom stew with dumplings **149**

e

eggs
    asparagus ends soup with soft boiled egg
        and cress topping **37**
    courgette, pea, red pepper
        and goat's cheese frittata **53**
    Mediterranean layered savoury
        bread-and-butter bake with feta **41**
    miso ramen with mushrooms, pickled red
        cabbage and soy-soaked eggs **103**
    Singapore noodles with egg scramble **26**
    veggie sausage and beans in spicy tomato sauce
        with baked eggs, feta and coriander **50**
equipment **10**

f

'faux duck' hoisin **131**, **205**
fennel: sweet potato, spring cabbage
    and fennel pot **29**
feta
    Mediterranean layered savoury
        bread-and-butter bake **41**
    veggie sausage and beans
        in spicy tomato sauce **50**
freezing **10–11**
frittata: courgette, pea, red pepper
    and goat's cheese **53**, **193**

g

garlic
    hunter's rice with wild garlic **42**
    lentil and garlic stew topped with chilli oil **108**
    slow-cooked cherry tomatoes with garlic **61**
goulash **128**, **204**
Greek-style stuffed peppers with rice
    and tomatoes **90**, **199**
gremolata topping **161**

h

harissa: sweet potato, spring cabbage
    and fennel pot **29**

herbs **7–8**

hob and oven cooking **188–211**

hoisin 'faux duck' **131**

hunter's rice with wild garlic **42**, **191**

i

Indonesian-style summer rice pot **82**, **198**

Irish stew **162**, **210**

Italian ribollita **170**, **211**

j

jackfruit

    marrow and jackfruit casserole with cider, baby onions and apple **107**

    slow-cooked BBQ jackfruit with slaw **69**

Jerusalem artichoke and potato stew with clementine and parsley gremolata topping **161**

k

kale

    lentil and garlic stew topped with chilli oil **108**

    Portuguese-style potato and three greens soup **165**

Kashmiri veggie mince curry with cucumber pickle **178**, **212**

katsu curry, spring veg **49**, **192**

Korean spicy sauce with pak choi and noodles **81**, **197**

l

lasagne: squash, mushroom and spinach **119**, **203**

leeks

    braised leeks, courgettes, spring carrots and tarragon **46**

    Irish stew **162**

    leek and pink peppercorn risotto with Shropshire blue **150**, **208**

    leek and potato chunky soup with Stilton toasties **154**, **208**

    Middle-Eastern chickpea stew **136**

    summer vegetables *au vin* topped with gherkins **77**

lemons

    butter beans in harissa and tahini sauce with dill **86**

    sweet potato, spring cabbage and fennel pot with harissa **29**

lentils

    chunky 'roots' soup **116**

    Irish stew **162**

    lentil and garlic stew topped with chilli oil **108**, **201**

    lentils and veggie sausages in romesco-style sauce **112**, **202**

    moussaka stew **115**

    mulligatawny pot **181**

    pottage pie **174**

m

mac and cheese with butternut squash **153**, **208**

Malaysian-style curry with sambal, aubergine and okra **34**, **190**

mangoes

    Caribbean sunshine stew **74**

    dried fruit pilaf **139**

marrow and jackfruit casserole with cider, baby onions and apple **107**, **201**

Mediterranean layered savoury bread-and-butter bake with feta **41**, **191**

Middle-Eastern chickpea stew **136**, **206**

mince

    Kashmiri veggie mince curry with cucumber pickle **178**

    Persian-style veggie mince **124**

minestrone: spring green with orzo pasta **30**

miso ramen with mushrooms, pickled red cabbage and soy-soaked eggs **103**, **200**

moussaka **115**, **202**

mulligatawny pot **181**, **212**

mung bean and paneer curry **205**

mushrooms

    Irish stew **162**

    miso ramen with mushrooms, pickled red cabbage and soy-soaked eggs **103**

    mushroom ragu with pappardelle **206**

    portobello mushroom stew with dumplings **149**, **207**

    ragu with pappardelle **140**

    squash, mushroom and spinach lasagne **119**

    Thai green curry **25**

    vegetable goulash **128**

    Vietnamese tofu pot with basil and mint **73**

n

new potato and asparagus pot with goat's cheese **21**, **188**

noodles

    Korean spicy sauce with pak choi and noodles **81**, **197**

    miso ramen with mushrooms, pickled red cabbage and soy-soaked eggs **103**, **20**

    Singapore noodles with egg scramble **26**

    sticky Japanese sauce with vegetables and noodles **94**, **200**

o

okra: Malaysian-style curry with sambal, aubergine and okra **34**

olives: Provençal green beans, olive and tomato **93**

orzo: spring green minestrone **30**

oven and hob cooking **188–212**

p

pak choi: Korean spicy sauce with pak choi and noodles **81**

paneer

    mung bean and paneer curry **132**

    sweet pepper and pea paneer curry **97**

parsnips

    chunky 'roots' soup **116**

    mulligatawny pot **181**

    parsnip and carrot tagine with ginger and rhubarb topping **157**, **209**

    vegetable goulash **128**

    whole 'roast' cauliflower and root vegetables **182**

pasta

    mac and cheese with butternut squash **153**

    mushroom ragu with pappardelle **140**, **206**

    spring green minestrone with orzo pasta **30**

    squash, mushroom and spinach lasagne **119**

pearl barley: risotto with courgette and tomato **33**, **190**

peas

    hunter's rice with wild garlic **42**

    sweet pepper and pea paneer curry **97**

    Thai green curry **25**

    yellow split pea soup with yoghurt and toasted almonds **173**

peppers

    Caribbean sunshine stew with mango **74**

    chunky Spanish stew **62**

    courgette, pea, red pepper and goat's cheese frittata **53**

    Greek-style stuffed peppers with rice and tomatoes **90**

    Indonesian-style summer rice pot **82**

Singapore noodles with egg scramble **26**
smoky peppers and potatoes
    with toasted almonds **58**
sweet pepper and pea paneer curry **97**
Persian-style veggie mince **124**, **204**
pilaf: brown rice and soya
    in a sweet Asian sauce **38**, **191**
pineapple: Indonesian-style summer rice pot **82**
polenta: black-eyed beans spicy pot
    with polenta dumplings **177**
Polish pickle soup **127**, **204**
Portuguese-style potato
    and three greens soup **165**, **210**

potatoes
    asparagus ends soup with soft boiled egg
        and cress topping **37**
    chunky Spanish stew **62**
    Irish stew **162**
    Jerusalem artichoke and potato stew
        with clementine and parsley
        gremolata topping **161**
    Kashmiri veggie mince curry
        with cucumber pickle **178**
    leek and potato chunky soup
        with Stilton toasties **154**
    moussaka **115**
    mulligatawny pot **181**
    new potato and asparagus pot
        with goat's cheese **21**, **188**
    perfect jacket spuds **100**
    Polish pickle soup **127**
    portobello mushroom stew with dumplings **149**
    Portuguese-style potato
        and three greens soup **165**
    smoky peppers and potatoes

    with toasted almonds **58**
    squash and potato dauphinoise **135**
    vegetable goulash **128**
    whole 'roast' cauliflower and root vegetables **182**
pottage pie **174**, **211**
protein **7**
Provençal green beans, olive and tomato **93**, **199**

prunes
    dried fruit pilaf **139**
    tempeh stew with sherry vinegar,
        star anise and prunes **146**
pulses, dried **7–8**
pumpkin, chestnuts, green chilli
    and cinnamon stew **104**, **201**

r

radishes, pickled **94**
ragu, mushroom **140**, **206**
raita: saffron rice with asparagus and dill raita **22**
ramen: miso with mushrooms, pickled red cabbage
    and soy-soaked eggs **103**
red cabbage with ginger beer topped
    with dates and Stilton **169**, **211**
red Thai tofu curry **53**, **193**
rhubarb: parsnip and carrot tagine
    with ginger and rhubarb topping **157**
ribollita, Italian **170**, **211**

rice
    brown rice and soya pilaf
        in a sweet Asian sauce **38**, **191**
    dried fruit pilaf **139**
    Greek-style stuffed peppers
        with rice and tomatoes **90**
    hunter's rice with wild garlic **42**, **191**
    Indonesian-style summer rice pot **82**, **198**
    leek and pink peppercorn risotto

    with Shropshire blue **150**

    perfect rice in the slow cooker **14**

    saffron rice with asparagus and dill raita **22**, **188**

    superfood rice, grain and bean pot
        with nori seaweed and avocado **84**

risotto

    leek and pink peppercorn risotto
        with Shropshire blue **150**, **208**

    pearl barley risotto
        with courgette and tomato **33**, **190**

s

safety **8**

saffron rice with asparagus and dill raita **22**, **188**

sambal: Malaysian-style curry
    with sambal, aubergine and okra **34**

sausages

    lentils and veggie sausages
        in romesco-style sauce **112**

    veggie sausage and beans in spicy tomato sauce
        with baked eggs, feta and coriander **50**, **193**

seasoning **7**

seaweed: superfood rice, grain and bean pot
    with nori and avocado **84**

Singapore noodles with egg scramble **26**, **189**

slaw: slow-cooked BBQ jackfruit with slaw **69**

slow cookers **11–13**, **16–17**

smoky peppers and potatoes
    with toasted almonds **58**, **194**

soups

    asparagus ends
        with soft boiled egg and cress topping **191**

    beetroot, orange and rosemary **145**, **207**

    cauliflower cheese with pickled walnuts **111**

    chunky 'roots' **116**, **203**

    leek and potato with Stilton toasties **154**

    mulligatawny pot **181**, **212**

    Polish pickle **127**, **204**

    Portuguese-style potato
        and three greens **165**, **210**

    spring carrot and chives **45**, **192**

    spring green minestrone with orzo pasta **30**, **190**

    sweetcorn chowder **88**, **199**

    yellow split pea
        with yoghurt and toasted almonds **173**, **211**

soya beans: brown rice
    and soya pilaf in a sweet Asian sauce **38**

spices **7–8**

spinach

    squash, mushroom and spinach lasagne **119**

    summer vegetables *au vin* topped
        with gherkins **77**

spring carrot and chives soup **45**, **192**

spring veg katsu curry **49**, **192**

sprouts, red onion and garlic
    with a lemon and tahini dressing **166**, **210**

squash

    black bean and squash stew
        with chipotle and sour cream drizzle **120**

    mac and cheese with butternut squash **153**

    pumpkin, chestnuts, green chilli
        and cinnamon stew **104**, **201**

    squash, mushroom and spinach lasagne **119**, **203**

    squash and potato dauphinoise **135**, **205**

sticky Japanese sauce
    with vegetables and noodles **94**

stock **7**

summer vegetables *au vin* topped
    with gherkins **77**, **197**

superfood rice, grain and bean pot **198**

swede: Middle-Eastern chickpea stew **136**

sweet potatoes

    Caribbean sunshine stew with mango **74**

chunky 'roots' soup **116**

parsnip and carrot tagine
    with ginger and rhubarb topping **157**

pottage pie **174**

spring cabbage and fennel pot
    with harissa and lemon **29**, **18**

sweetcorn

    chowder **88**, **199**

    sticky Japanese sauce
        with vegetables and noodles **94**

t

tagine: parsnip and carrot
    with ginger and rhubarb topping **157**

tempeh stew with sherry vinegar,
    star anise and prunes **146**, **207**

Thai curries

    green **25**, **189**

    red tofu curry **54**, **193**

Vietnamese tofu pot with basil and mint **73**

timings **10**

tofu

    red Thai tofu curry **54**

    Vietnamese tofu pot with basil and mint **73**

tomatoes

    aubergine and tomato stew **70**

    chickpea balls in tomato sauce **120**

    courgette and tomato Provençal tian **61**

    Greek-style stuffed peppers
        with rice and tomatoes **90**

    Korean spicy sauce with pak choi and noodles **81**

    Malaysian-style curry
        with sambal, aubergine and okra **34**

    pearl barley risotto with courgette and tomato **33**

    Provençal green beans, olive and tomato **93**

    slow-cooked cherry tomatoes with garlic **61**

    stuffed aubergines
        with fresh tomato and parsley **78**

    veggie sausage and beans
        in spicy tomato sauce **50**

turnips: Irish stew **162**

v

vegetable goulash **128**, **204**

Vietnamese tofu pot with basil and mint **73**, **196**

w

whole 'roast' cauliflower and root vegetables **212**

wild rice **14**

y

yoghurt

    saffron rice with asparagus and dill raita **22**

    sweet potato, spring cabbage and fennel pot **29**

PENGUIN MICHAEL JOSEPH

UK | USA | Canada | Ireland | Australia
India | New Zealand | South Africa

Penguin Michael Joseph is part of the Penguin Random House group of companies whose addresses can be found at global.penguinrandomhouse.com

First published 2025
001

Text copyright © Heather Whinney, 2025
Photography copyright © William Shaw, 2025
The moral right of the author has been asserted

Set in Qanelas Soft
Design by Gail Jones, Sarah Fraser, Dan Prescott-Bennett, Nikki Ellis
Colour reproduction by Altalmage Ltd
Printed and bound in Vietnam by RRD

The authorized representative in the EEA is Penguin Random House Ireland, Morrison Chambers, 32 Nassau Street, Dublin D02 YH68

A CIP catalogue record for this book is available from the British Library

ISBN: 978–0–241–67251–8

www.greenpenguin.co.uk

Penguin Random House is committed to a sustainable future for our business, our readers and our planet. This book is made from Forest Stewardship Council® certified paper.